THE LEGEND OF SEYAVASH

Ferdowsi *(c.* 940–*c.* 1020) was born and died in a village near Tus, in Khorasan (north-eastern Iran). He belonged to the small landed gentry of his region, a class that saw itself as the custodian of Iran's ancient traditions. During his lifetime Iran gradually became independent of the caliphate in Baghdad, and Ferdowsi's epic *Shahnameh,* a retelling of the history of his country from the creation of the world to the seventh-century Arab invasion, was a product of this new sense of independence. Legend has it that Ferdowsi's poem was ignored by the Turkish ruler, Mahmud of Ghazni, who conquered Khorasan, and that after spending most of his life on his masterpiece the poet died a poor and embittered man.

ABOLQASEM FERDOWSI

THE
LEGEND OF SEYAVASH

TRANSLATED WITH AN INTRODUCTION AND NOTES BY
DICK DAVIS

MAGE PUBLISHERS
WASHINGTON, DC
2004

Library of Congress Cataloging-in-Publication Data

Firdawsī.
[Siyāvush. English]
The legend of Seyavash / Abolqasem Ferdowsi ; translated with an
introduction and notes by Dick Davis.-- Rev. ed.
p. cm.
Includes bibliographical references.
ISBN 0-934211-91-4 (pbk. : alk. paper)
I. Davis, Dick, 1945- II. Title.
PK6456.A12S5913 2004
891'.5511--dc22
2004005356

New Revised Edition
Printed in the USA

PAPERBACK ISBN 0-934211-91-4

MAGE BOOKS ARE AVAILABLE AT BOOKSTORES OR DIRECTLY FROM THE
PUBLISHER. VISIT MAGE ON THE WEB AT WWW.MAGE.COM OR CALL
1 800 962 0922, OR E-MAIL INFO@MAGE.COM

TO AFKHAM,
AND TO OUR CHILDREN MARIAM AND MEHRI

CONTENTS

INTRODUCTION

The Legend of Seyavash is a section of *The Shahnameh,* written by the Persian poet Ferdowsi *(c.* 940-*c.* 1020). *The Shahnameh* bears approximately the same relation to Persian culture as the works of Homer do to ancient Greek culture. Coming at the virtual beginning of the recorded literature, it is seen as a massive and masterly work and, in some sense, as a touchstone for everything subsequent to it. It is also considered a uniquely accurate icon of the culture that it defines and, by influencing the notion of self-identity it bequeaths to its people, that it moulds. As Alessandro Bausani has written, Ferdowsi has been regarded by modern Persians as 'the symbol of Persianness, the father of his country,'[1] and, though this may be less generally true since the Islamic Revolution of 1979, the remark still has a broad validity to it.

As with Homer's work, the style of the poem indicates a long oral tradition behind the written version we now read, and the subject matter is largely the heroic history of the people celebrated in the poem. We are dealing, then, with a national epic. But it is a national epic far vaster in scope than any of its Western equivalents, concerned as it is with the history of Iran[2] from the creation of the world to the Arab/Islamic conquest of the country in the seventh century AD. Perhaps the only works of comparable scope in world literature are the Indian epics, the *Mahabharata* and *Ramayana.* In sheer size, if nothing else, Ferdowsi's achievement is extraordinary, and it has been estimated that *The Shahnameh* is probably the longest poem (some 50,000 lines—very long lines at that, approximately equal to the length of a heroic couplet in English) known to have been substantially completed by one man.[3] The Seyavash episode translated here is a little over 2,500 lines, and it therefore represents only a small portion of the poem, though it is certainly one of its best-known and best-written episodes.

It is usual to divide *The Shahnameh* (for convenience's sake: these are divisions made by modern commentators, not by the poet himself) into three sections—the mythological section, with which the poem opens, the legendary section, and the quasi-historical section, with which it closes. The mythological section is in many ways more like a cosmogony than an epic, recalling, for a Western reader, Hesiod rather than Homer: it details the creation of the world and of the first man, the origin of evil and of human strife, and the discovery/invention of the arts of civilization. The first man is also the first king of the world—a Persian Adam called Keyumars—and it is significant that, though Ferdowsi was undoubtedly a sincere Muslim, he begins his poem in this way (with a king and a figure from Persian myth), rather than by drawing on the version of the world's and man's creation offered in the Koran.

The middle, legendary section of the poem (from which our story is taken) is the one that corresponds most closely to Western notions of epic poetry. More or less constant warfare between Iran and its northern neighbor Turan is described;[4] and the overt values the poem promotes are those typical of epic poetry the world over—fierce loyalty to tribe and king, bravery, military prowess and the ability to trick the enemy (the epithet of one of the heroes is the equivalent of Odysseus' 'guileful'). In this section Ferdowsi inherits an amalgamation of two quite separate epic traditions—that of the Iranians and that of the inhabitants of Sistan (approximately southwestern Afghanistan). The family that rules Sistan is nominally subject to the Iranian royal family and provides them with their main champions; there is, however, a constant and subtle rivalry between the two clans and it is this rivalry which generates many of the best-known stories of the poem. The great hero of Sistan is Rostam (made famous in the West by Matthew Arnold's version of the story of Sohrab and Rostam, in which Rostam inadvertently kills his son)[5] and Rostam is seen as the counselor, champion and savior of the Iranian kings. Some of these kings can act with extraordinary foolishness (e.g. Kavus, who is the king during the Seyavash episode) or malevolence (e.g. Goshtasp, who tries to have Rostam enslaved), and when there is such a conflict the reader's sympathy is always directed towards Rostam rather than towards his nominal overlord. The overt value of loyalty to the king come what may still prevails, but much of the poem's human interest arises from the poet's/audience's perception of how difficult it can be to maintain such loyalty, given the nature of some of the kings who demand it Late on in the poem a king asks his advisor, 'Who is the most desperate of men?', and the answer is, 'A good man whose king is a fool', the remark neatly encapsulating the problem many of the poem's heroes face, including our hero Seyavash.

It is in this legendary section of the poem that we realize that our modern Western perception of Iran/Persia differs radically from the one offered by Ferdowsi. The poet is utilizing the ethnic inheritance of the Iranian people, originally a tribe or tribes inhabiting central Asia who descended on to the Iranian plateau and into modern Persia at some time before the beginning of recorded history. The landscape of much of *The Shahnameh* is the grassy steppe of central Asia, not the arid desert of central Persia, and almost all the place names mentioned in the first two thirds of the poem are not now within the confines of Iran. In the section here translated we read of Merv (now in Turkmenistan) and Balkh (now in northern Afghanistan), and the border between 'Iran' and 'Turan' is the river Oxus. The place-names we associate with Persia—Fars, Shiraz, Hamadan, Esfahan, Yazd—are virtually absent until the last third of the poem and only appear with any frequency in the last section. In the first two thirds the centre of Persian civilization and influence is seen as what is now the extreme north-eastern corner of the country, Khorasan, where the poet was born, which then extended deep into Central Asian and Afghan territory. Fars (Pars, from which we derive the word Persia), which the West as a result of the ancient Greek obsession with the Achaemenid empire, has always seen as the cradle of Persian civilization, does not appear in the poem except as a distant province until just before the advent of Alexander the Great.

The 'historical' section of the poem does not correspond very closely to the West's notions of Persian history either. The Achaemenids are virtually absent; Alexander (Eskandar) is half-Persian, having been born from a Greek princess and a Persian royal father; the Seleucids and Parthians, who between them ruled

Iran for about five hundred years, are hardly mentioned. The vast majority of the lines dealing with the history of Iran after the conquest by Eskandar are concerned with the Sasanians, the dynasty destroyed by the Arab invasion in the 640s, and via whom Ferdowsi must have received most of his sources. The great heroic figure of the closing section of the poem is the Sasanian king Anushirvan the Just, who is balanced, in the legendary portion of the poem, by the exemplary king Khosrow (the son of Seyavash).

The Sasanian bias of the later portions of the poem has also radically affected the way in which the mythological and legendary sections are presented. In a way, it is the Sasanian version of the Iranian identity and history which Ferdowsi inherits and to a large extent transmits. This is especially noticeable in two areas—religion and politics. The Sasanian religion was a modified form of Zoroastrianism, a faith deriving from the prophet Zoroaster, who probably lived in Iran at some time in the seventh century BC, though a date much earlier than this is claimed by some, notably by the distinguished scholar of ancient Iranian religions, Mary Boyce. For our purposes the most important aspect of Zoroastrianism is its dualism: the universe is a battleground between the forces of good and evil, both being represented by a divine principle—Ahura Mazda for the good (and light) and Ahriman for the evil (and darkness). The soul of man is a microcosm of the universal battlefield and each man must choose between the contending forces. A Zoroastrian heretic, Mani, gave the West the Manichean religion, which developed the Zoroastrian dualism into a system that ended by rejecting the physical world as belonging to the realm of Ahriman, the realm of the spirit being that of Ahura Mazda.

Though such an extreme rejection of physical reality is not part of the original Zoroastrian message, a suspicion of appearances and physical reality as being somehow less 'good' (even less 'true') than the spiritual realm left its legacy to later Zoroastrianism and, via his Sasanian sources, on Ferdowsi's poem. Ferdowsi's poem has, in contrast with almost all other epics, an urgently ethical cast to it, and this derives in large part from the notion that the true battle, of which all other battles are, as it were, emblems in transient physical reality, is that being waged between good and evil. As important as the physical battles with swords and spears in Ferdowsi's work are the inward ones that take place in the souls of the heroes, and this is particularly true in what are probably the two finest stories of the poem—those of Seyavash and Esfandyar. This inwardness at the poem's high points is something that sharply demarcates it from the notion of the heroic we derive from Homer: Erich Auerbach's famous remarks about 'clearly outlined, brightly and uniformly illuminated men and things [that] stand out in a realm where everything is visible' characterizing Homeric epic are quite beside the point for Ferdowsi's poem. In the poem's greatest episodes we feel that Ferdowsi is interested primarily in moral, inward and often hidden, rather than physical heroism, and one of his favorite verbs is a word describing mental 'writhing', the torments of conscience and regret. The overwhelming duty of the poem's heroes is to do what is right, and this rightness is not necessarily consonant with the victory of one's own side in battle or the survival of one's own people, as is the case in a more straightforward heroic poem. Further, failure in the 'real' physical world is not incompatible with triumph in the moral and spiritual world—as is the case with Seyavash, who triumphs spiritually only to be destroyed physically. Again we are far removed from the world of Homer, where failure is failure pure and simple, or even that of so ethical a poet as Virgil, for whom Aeneas' spiritual triumph must also mean literal physical triumph.

The second significant legacy of the Sasanian world-view to the poem is the central importance given to the notion of kingship, a legacy passed on to much of subsequent Persian culture, arguably largely by means of *The Shahnameh* itself. This notion of the central importance of the 'Great King' we know to have been important to the Achaemenids too—it was largely how the Greeks defined their difference from the Persians, and in writers like Herodotus and Xenophon we can see the kind of appalled fascination with which the Greeks regarded this Persian phenomenon. But it was with the Sasanians, who derived from the old Achaemenid centre of Iran, Fars, and who seem consciously to have revived Achaemenid claims to imperial glory, that it entered into its most complex and theologically sanctioned development. The Great King was the representative of Ahura Mazda on earth; he ruled by divine right and possessed a glory unique to kings (the royal *farr*) conferred on him by God. The Sasanian kings ruled in seclusion from their people, surrounded by an aura of divine power. To rebel was to rebel against God. The very survival of the country was dependent on the survival of the king and his family and when a new king acceded to the throne the world itself was seen as renewed. All this The *Shahnameh* faithfully reflects, and the very name of the poem (which means 'King-Book') indicates the centrality of this concept to the work.

The weight of such authority, both secular and spiritual, might be thought to have a monolithic and deadening effect on the values of the poem. But in reality almost the contrary is true. The demands on a subject's allegiance are indeed overwhelming, but they are often split between contradictory claims. What the king demands and what God or the conscience (or even simple common sense) demand should theoretically be one and the same thing, but they are frequently at variance, and this dilemma of loyalty is faced at one time or another by most of the poem's heroes.

The claims of God and king are shadowed by a third source of authority, that of the father over the son. It is a striking fact that in the three best-known stories of the legendary section of the poem— those of Sohrab, Seyavash and Esfandyar—a son is killed as a direct result of his father's actions. Rostam kills his son Sohrab in ignorance and with his own hands; Kavus and Goshtasp (the fathers of Seyavash and Esfandyar respectively) make demands on their sons which they cannot in all conscience fulfill. Seyavash rejects his father's demand and throws himself on the mercy of his country's traditional enemies who ultimately kill him; Esfandyar reluctantly attempts to fulfill his father's order that he enslave Rostam and is killed in the process. The fact that Rostam does not know it is his own son whom he kills in combat (on the orders of king Kavus) is what enables him to kill him at all; but the message that the episode conveys, that the father kills the son, is one that is then repeated in the stories of Seyavash and Esfandyar, whose fathers are ultimately responsible for their deaths even though they are not their immediate cause. In the *Farsnameh* of Ebn Balkhi, a prose work written in the twelfth century and reproducing some of the same material as Ferdowsi's *Shahnameh*, Seyavash's father, Kavus, exclaims after his son's death, 'It was I who killed the pure-souled Seyavash, not

Afrasyab', and though Ferdowsi's Kavus is too unaware of his own folly to say such a thing, the audience draws the same conclusion. When Esfandyar is slain in *The Shahnameh*, his dying words blame his father, and not the actual opponent in combat who has dealt him the death-blow (Rostam), for his death, and his whole family unite with him in ascribing the blame to Goshtasp.

Seyavash and Esfandyar are presented almost entirely as victims of others' machinations, and Sohrab too is Rostam's victim albeit an unintended one. Similarly many of the kings' champions—and this is especially true of the poem's greatest champion, Rostam— are presented as the victims of their kings' machinations and/or foolishness, and, indeed, Rostam's family is finally wiped out by the Iranian royal family. Beside the weight of authority demanding absolute obedience (the authority of God, king and father), a different ethic emerges, which centers on a sympathy for the victims of such authority. We cannot doubt that we are meant to sympathize with Seyavash in his conflict with his king and father Kavus, and with Rostam in his conflict with the king Goshtasp, who tries to enslave him. The poem's depiction of authority is profoundly ambiguous: it is seen as a prerequisite of organized human life in general, and of the survival of the Iranian nation in particular, but it is also considered the cause of human tragedy and suffering, and the various embodiments of authority in the poem are among its least attractive characters. This questioning seems, in a baffled way, even to extend to the authority of God/Fate itself—and Ferdowsi's comments *in propria persona* at various points in his poem where he has to record the tragic death of a character he admires hint at this; one of the most striking of these comments occurs after Seyavash is killed, when the poet says in effect that he can't imagine what God can be thinking of by arranging matters thus.

Ferdowsi finished *The Shahnameh* in 1010 and claimed to have spent most of his adult life working on the poem—a claim which, given its vast length, is entirely believable. This means that the poem was written in the latter half of the tenth century and the opening years of the eleventh and though, dealing as it does with prehistoric and quasi-historic material, its roots extend into the distant past, it is also a product specifically of its own time.

Since the Arab/Muslim conquest of Iran in the mid seventh century the country had been part of the Islamic caliphate ruled first from Damascus, under the Umayyads (661–750), and then from Baghdad, under the Abbasids. The Abbasid revolt against Umayyad rule drew particular strength from Khorasan, and many Persians were involved in the movement. Nevertheless, though it is true that Persians were no longer the wholly peripheral people they had been under the Umayyads and that they had great influence at the Abbasid court (for example through the Barmecide family of civil servants), Iran was at first still seen as a group of provinces subject to an Arab, and therefore alien, family's rule. During the later Abbasid period, within which Ferdowsi's lifetime fell, the eastern provinces especially began to achieve something like *de facto* independence of Baghdad, though they were still nominally subject to the caliph there. Under the Samanids—client kings of the Abbasid caliphate—in particular, who ruled in the north-east, a Persian cultural renaissance began to take place. The language of the court became Persian rather than Arabic, and, most importantly, Persian became the language of court poetry. The Samanid princes prided themselves on their Persian identity and encouraged a local and national antiquarianism that emphasized the length and uniqueness of the Persian past. Ferdowsi belonged to the *dehqan* (small landed gentry) class, which was seen as a repository of local tradition and legend and he records during the course of his poem how he conscientiously collected the stories of his country's past, how a particular history that had been recently commissioned was given to him as a major source, and how he sought out those who could pass on oral traditions to him. One reason that Khorasan (rather than the Fars of the Achaemenids) is the cradle of Persian civilization in *The Shahnameh* is that the poem was written there and drew on local tradition.

The Shahnameh was a direct product of the reappearance of a sense of Persian ethnic identity and, as with most epics, the people celebrated are defined as being in conflict with their neighbors, with whom they do not share ethnicity. The first act of human evil in the poem is carried out by an Arab, who seizes power from the Persian king, Jamshid, and the poem ends with the conquest of Iran by the victorious Arab armies of Islam. But if the poem is framed by an ambiguous hostility to Arab civilization (ambiguous because though it destroyed Persian independence it also brought Islam, considered by virtually all of Ferdowsi's contemporary fellow-countrymen as the true religion, to the country), most of it is taken up with the rivalry between Iran and its northern neighbor, Turan, whose inhabitants are Turks. Unfortunately for Ferdowsi the Samanid renaissance of independent Persian culture was short-lived, and eastern Iran was conquered during the poet's lifetime by Mahmud of Ghazni (in Afghanistan), an ethnic Turk. The prestige of Persian culture had spread to Mahmud's court and he was an assiduous patron of Persian poetry; nevertheless, it is difficult to see how he could have been particularly interested in a poem like *The Shahnameh,* which celebrated countless Persian victories over the Turks and which usually cast the Turks as evil and their kings as representatives of the evil principle of the universe, Ahriman. And, indeed, the legends concerning Ferdowsi's presentation of his poem to his new ruler record that Mahmud was singularly unimpressed by it and that Ferdowsi retired to his village in Khorasan a neglected and embittered man. Some manuscripts of *The Shahnameh* include a satire, which may or may not be genuine, on Mahmud and his stinginess toward the poet. All the manuscripts contain passages in which Ferdowsi proclaims his pride in his achievement, and all include passages lamenting his lack of reward for his life's work.

Though the Seyavash story is a more or less self-contained narrative, framed by comments from the poet *in propria persona* (Ferdowsi's normal way of showing when an episode begins and ends), it is also a section of the continuing narrative of the poem as a whole, and a brief summary of the events in *The Shahnameh* prior to the opening of the Seyavash episode will make parts of the story plainer.

The poem opens with praise of God, wisdom, the prophet Muhammad, the caliph Ali and Sultan Mahmud of Ghazni, from whom Ferdowsi clearly hoped for patronage, together with a short section on how he came by his main written source, and one on his predecessor, the poet Daqiqi. We then pass to the creation of the world, to the first king, Keyumars, and his struggle against the forces of evil represented by demons. This struggle is carried on by his descendants Hushang, Tahmoures and Jamshid. Jamshid is a Promethean figure who introduces the arts of civilization to mankind and who thinks that his power rivals God's. His hubris is punished by the arrival of the Arab demon-king Zahhak, who kills Jamshid and sets up a reign of great rapacity and cruelty; snakes grow from his shoulders and the only food they will accept is the brains of young Persians. Zahhak is overthrown by a popular uprising led by the blacksmith Kaveh, and Kaveh's blacksmith's apron becomes the banner of the legendary Persian kings. Kaveh is joined by the prince Faridun, who rules the world with justice. Faridun divides his inheritance between his three sons, Tur, Salm and Iraj. Tur is given Asia, Salm the West, and the youngest, Iraj, is given the land of Iran. Tur and Salm plot against their brother, who is represented as a naive and well-meaning innocent, and kill him. Manuchehr, a grand-son of Iraj, avenges his grandfather's murder and rules in Iran. From this time on Iran and Turan (ruled by Tur and his descendants, in particular the king Afrasyab, who is king of Turan during the Seyavash episode) are more or less perpetually at war. During the reign of the weak and corrupt Persian king Nozar, Afrasyab invades and pillages Iran, and Nozar is killed. There is an interregnum during which Rostam and his father Zal more or less run the country; finally they invite Qobad to be king. Qobad restores the country's fortunes, driving out Afrasyab and his forces and ruling justly and well. However, Qobad's son is the incompetent and rash king Kavus, who is Seyavash's father and the king of Iran when our story opens.

Ferdowsi devotes more space to the reign of Kavus than to that of any other monarch, with the possible exception of Anushirvan the Just.[6] That he should give such a flawed and unsatisfactory king such prominence in his poem is a strong indication that we should not consider it a work written wholly in praise of kings and the notion of kingship, as it has often been regarded. Indeed, the most interesting and aesthetically telling episodes of the poem[7] virtually all deal with weak, evil or corrupt kings, and the Seyavash story is no exception.

The irascible instability of Kavus's character has already been demonstrated at least four times before the opening of the Seyavash episode. Contrary to the advice of his ministers he attacks Mazanderan, the home of demons under their leader the *Div-e Sepid* ('The White Demon). The *Div-e Sepid* captures Kavus, and Rostam has to be sent to rescue him. Kavus also goes courting, and is imprisoned by his new father-in-law, the king of Hamaveran. Again, Rostam has to be sent to rescue him. Kavus then decides to build himself a flying machine, drawn aloft by eagles—this crashes in enemy territory and again Rostam is sent to bring the hapless king home. Rostam has a further reason to resent Kavus's authority: when Rostam had inadvertently mortally wounded his own son Sohrab, Kavus was in possession of a drug that could have saved the boy; he refused to give it to Rostam partly because he was afraid of Sohrab's prowess if he lived, but partly in order to punish Rostam for what Kavus considered the hero's insufficiently humble demeanor. By the time the Seyavash story opens Kavus has been firmly established in the audience's mind as foolish and short-tempered, often well-meaning but equally often vindictive, alternately vacillating and headstrong.

The Seyavash story is constructed with great symmetry and economy: there are two tests of the prince's integrity, both of which he passes successfully, and there are two plots against his life—the first fails and the second succeeds. The first test is against his sexual integrity, when his stepmother queen Sudabeh[8] attempts to seduce him. His resistance to Sudabeh's wiles and her subsequent fury against him remind a Western reader of the Hippolytus/Phaedra story and, as with Hippolytus, his integrity has something of an anguished adolescent flight from sexuality about it.[9] Having passed unscathed through the metaphorical fire of Sudabeh's passion for him, he is then required to pass through a literal mountain of fire in order to prove his innocence, which of course he is able to do. In order to get away from the corrupt atmosphere of the court he asks permission to lead the Persian armies against the invading forces of Turan, whom he defeats with the help of Rostam. He concludes a treaty with the king of Turan, Afrasyab, and takes hostages as a token of Afrasyab's good conduct. The second and far more important test of his integrity comes when his king and father, Kavus, orders him to send the hostages to the Persian court where they will be killed. Seyavash feels unable to do this in good conscience and throws himself on the mercy of his country's enemies. Afrasyab welcomes him, and marries him first to the daughter of his chief minister and then to his own daughter. But the plot by Sudabeh against Seyavash at the Persian court is paralleled by a plot by Afrasyab's brother against Seyavash at the Turanian court. Sexually unsuccessful with Seyavash, Sudabeh accuses him of sexual treachery; Afrasyab's brother was the commander of the armies of Turan defeated by Seyavash and, militarily unsuccessful against Seyavash, he accuses him of military treachery, of planning a military coup. Seyavash is unable to refute the calumny, largely because of his innocent trust in those who have plotted against him, and is killed. His second wife, the daughter of Afrasyab, is pregnant with the future king, Kay Khosrow, and is saved by Afrasyab's minister, Piran. Kay Khosrow is brought up in secret, escapes to Iran and eventually returns to avenge his father's murder. The story sounds and is fairly complex, but one is never aware of strain as one reads— the poet keeps the various characters in play with an ease which is so practiced and elegant as to seem instinctive, and in the unfolding of events he is able to embody with force and emotional conviction the ethical preoccupations that run through so much of his poem.

In a work of the length of *The Shahnameh* it is only natural that one should feel that the poet's interest is quickened more by some episodes than by others. As Ferdowsi's sources no longer exist it is often difficult to guess whether a particularly strong delineation is the result of his own interest or whether it is something he has inherited. However, there are histories[10] roughly contemporary with Ferdowsi's poem which deal with much the same material, and when we compare their treatment of particular incidents with Ferdowsi's we do notice a difference. The poet is clearly more interested in stories that emphasize moral heroism than are the historians, and a concomitant of this is that he lavishes attention on episodes that deal with inward conflict—whether it be conflict within Iran itself between different sources of power, within the royal family, or within a given hero's soul and conscience. He is also far more interested in something that approaches the Western notion of tragedy—the notion of noble souls ineluctably destroyed partly by flaws in their own characters and partly by external events over which they have no control. The tragic and ethical aspects of episodes are, in the writings of his historian near-contemporaries, firmly subordinated to dynastic and national concerns. In Ferdowsi's work, however, they often seem completely to take over the foreground of the poet's—and thus his audience's—consciousness, and the dynastic concerns, while always present as a ground bass, become temporarily subordinate. In the Seyavash story the hero chooses to side with his country's enemy and his conscience rather than with his own country and what he sees as evil; his notion of the right is supranational, and while he does figure in the work of the historians it is only in Ferdowsi's poem, among extant texts, that the ethical, tragic and quasi-mystical implications of his decisions are explored with such earnestness and in such depth.

It is not normally to epic, among literary genres, that we look for psychological truth: the characters of epic tend to be types, icons, rather than individuals, and while we may feel that we 'know' Odysseus or Hector we do not expect the same psychological subtlety and intensity from their delineations as we do from the creations of, say, Henry James or Proust. In Ferdowsi too we can see a broad, rather than detailed, portrayal of character in most cases, and often the demands of plot will mean that a character's implied inward nature will shift slightly from episode to episode. A good example of this is the character of Sudabeh, Seyavash's stepmother: in the first episode in which she appears (when Kavus goes to her country in order to court her) she is portrayed as a loving, loyal consort; in the Seyavash episode she is a scheming hypocrite. It might be possible to construct a satisfactory psychological profile for her (e.g. her propensity to deceit is there from the beginning, as she deceives her father to save her husband), but it would probably be a wasted effort; her 'character' shifts as the course of the episodes in which she figures demands. Another example from our current story is the character of the king of Turan, Afrasyab: nowhere in the poem

is he presented as ethically attractive; however, in the Seyavash episode he is much less unattractive than elsewhere in the poem and
his attentive concern for Seyavash's safety is presented as genuine.
This is clearly in order to contrast him with his brother Garsivaz
and with king Kavus, who are the real villains of the piece.

But one way of recognizing Ferdowsi's particular interest in
a character is, I would suggest, the way that he does in fact give
him or her a psychological depth and reality beyond that which we
expect from the personages of epic. We have already seen how the
complex character of Kavus is treated with considerable consis-
tency throughout the many episodes in which he figures. Arguably
the same is true of the poem's most famous hero, Rostam, and
Seyavash's is a startlingly plausible psychological portrait—as is
perhaps appropriate for a character whose outward acts are so gov-
erned by inward, ethical preoccupations.

Seyavash's psychological reality is related to the theme of filicide
and fatherly oppression that runs through the poem, in that he is
presented as a character simultaneously in search of and in flight
from his father. He is not brought up by his real father, Kavus, but
by a surrogate father, Rostam; when he returns to Kavus's court
he is not familiar with his father's true character (as the audience
by this time is) and mistakenly trusts him when advised to visit
Sudabeh in the harem. When his conscience does rebel against his
true father's advice (that the hostages from Turan be sent to the
Persian court where they will be murdered), his instinct is to turn
to his surrogate father, Rostam. But Rostam has been relieved of his
command and is not available to the prince. Seyavash turns instead
to Piran, the counselor of Afrasyab, who advises him repeatedly to
think of Afrasyab as a father, and Piran too is described as his father.
Seyavash's progress can be seen as a turning from father-figure to
father-figure (Kavus, Rostam, Piran, Afrasyab); as he is betrayed
by his Iranian father Kavus, so he is betrayed by his Turanian
'father' Afrasyab; as the Iranian 'father' Rostam is absent when
most needed, so the Turanian 'father' Piran is absent when most
needed. His search for an adequate father who will both protect
him and support him ethically is reflected in the overriding claims
of his anguished superego, which demands absolute ethical integrity from him and finally leads him to trust the most potent but

also most absent father of all, God—who, like his earthly fathers, proves unwilling or unable to prevent his death. If all this sounds far too twentieth-century and Western an interpretation, we should remember that Freud claimed to have discovered nothing new and that everything he had to offer was present in the works of the poets before him. Indeed it may well be that one of the characteristics of a great narrative poet is exactly this intuitive ability to reproduce and reveal psychologically compelling behavior that appears to transcend cultural and temporal boundaries.

By the time one reaches the end of the Seyavash story, however, it is not perhaps the psychological aspect of it that has proved the most compelling. The story begins with the stuff of romance—a foreign girl of royal blood is found as a fugitive and is introduced into the king's harem. From this story-book beginning the tale turns realistic, particularly with the introduction of Sudabeh. She too, as a scheming stepmother, could be considered a figure from fairy-tale and romance, but her portrait has a fierce plausibility about it, largely because of the words she is given to speak, which establish her in the audience's mind as a potent, menacing reality. Seyavash's reactions to her and to his various 'fathers' continue this vein of realism, but it begins to dissolve with his trial by fire, and by the time he reaches Turan a strong supernatural element has taken over the tale. The emphasis shifts from the psychological to the 'spiritual' and supernatural, and this is particularly noticeable as soon as Seyavash has become established in Turan. He knows he is going to be killed unjustly, he prophesies the manner of his death and its results and he claims knowledge of the future and of God's will. The story becomes mythical rather than realistic, spiritual rather than psychological.

This mythical, spiritual side to the story was clearly a component from the beginning, or at least considerably preceded Ferdowsi's version. It is known that laments for the martyrdom of Seyavash were sung in central Asia before Ferdowsi ever put pen to paper, and such memorials have been performed up to the twentieth century in various parts of Iran. To an outsider the episode has strong similarities with the story of the martyrdom of Hosayn which is such a prominent feature of the beliefs of Shia Islam; in both cases a young and noble leader who is the hope of his people is cut down in his prime as a result of evil machinations against him; in both cases the victim is a symbol of triumph by martyrdom in that the future will vindicate the rights of the deceased. The shared emotional atmosphere of the two stories is a prominent feature of the Persian cultural experience and has had a lasting effect on Persian artistic expression.

A clue as to the possible mythical origins of the story may be found in the imagery Ferdowsi employs in his version. Like many epic writers, Ferdowsi is not a poet who particularly delights in startling or original imagery, and most of his tropes are formulae distributed apparently haphazardly throughout the poem as a whole. But the Seyavash episode is something of an exception to this rule, unified as it is by a series of images that run throughout the whole tale and which are rare elsewhere in the poem. The images are those of fire and water and, in particular, of fire and water as challenges to the hero. The most famous episode of the story, and the one that most attracted the miniaturists who embellished later manuscripts of *The Shahnameh*, is Seyavash's trial by fire after Sudabeh accuses him of the attempt on her chastity. But the trope occurs with some regularity throughout the whole tale; shortly before his death Seyavash dreams of being caught between fire and water; when Piran dreams of the birth of Kay Khosrow, Seyavash's son, the image is of a candle being lit from the sun; when Garsivaz deceitfully promises to help Seyavash he says he will put out the king's fire of wrath by the water of his advice. The reader will notice other examples of the image. Most interesting is the way the two elements are often associated, even when this can only be done by some contortion. A telling example of this is the description given of Seyavash's clothes when he emerges from the trial by fire unscathed: it is said that if the fire he had passed through had been water, his clothes would not have been wet. It may be that this rather peculiar image is a trace indicating that there were - at some point in the preliterate development of the story—two trials, one by fire and one by water. There is in any case a passage through water later in the poem: in the same way that Seyavash passes through fire after the attempt on his sexual integrity by Sudabeh, he passes through water (when he crosses the Oxus to enter the territory of Turan) after the attempt on his military integrity by his father (when ordered to hand over the hostages to their deaths). The story appears in origin to be one involving rites of passage, symbolized by passing through fire and water, to a higher spiritual state, culminating in the destruction of the body and the triumph of the spirit, the latter symbolized by the new generation as embodied in the hero's son, the unworldly Khosrow. The importance of fire and water in the beliefs of Zoroastrianism cannot be discounted here, but the story seems to refer back to an even more 'universal', perhaps shamanistic, period in which heroes representing the growth of the human soul in spiritual awareness are put to ritual spiritual and physical tests.

The Shahnameh has been known to the West, at least by name, since the seventeenth century; but it was only with the late-eighteenth-century orientalist Sir William Jones[11] that the poem was seriously read and studied in the West. Jones translated parts of the poem into Latin and planned a tragedy based on the Sohrab and Rostam episode. A verse translation of some episodes (into heroic couplets) was made by Joseph Champion in the late eighteenth century, and another into the same medium by James Atkinson in the early nineteenth (Atkinson also produced a shortened prose version of the entire mythological and legendary sections of the poem, ending with the appearance of Eskandar). Editions were produced first in Calcutta (where Jones had been a judge) and then in Leyden, and the first attempt at a complete translation into a European language was that by the German orientalist, Mohl. Mohl was an acquaintance of the Goncourt brothers and was resident in Paris in the middle years of the nineteenth century.[12] His (prose) translation was into French and was printed en face with his edition of the poem, which was not superseded until well into this century. Though modern scholarship has considerably revised Mohl's view of the text, and though a few errors can be found in his translation, his work is a quite remarkable monument of scholarship considering the limited materials at his disposal. His translation, which is vigorous and frequently provides very persuasive solutions to difficult parts of the text, can still be consulted with great profit.

A complete verse translation into Italian was made by Pizzi in the late nineteenth century. Pizzi's version was in 'versi sciolti', unrhymed hendecasyllabics, the Italian equivalent of blank verse, and in the Edwardian period a blank verse translation of the whole poem into English was begun by George and Edmond Warner, to be finally completed in 1925. It is perhaps unfortunate that this version can legitimately be called a 'Warner Brothers' epic, as it well lives up to the negative connotations the phrase suggests, though there are fine compensating moments in among the Edwardian Wardour Street diction. The most recent (prose) translation which covers the whole poem (though only by omitting considerable portions of it, including more than half of the Seyavash episode) is that by Reuben Levy, first published in 1967. Levy's view of the poem seems to have been that it was essentially a work about military prowess and kingly glory and, from the point of view of the themes prominent in the Seyavash episode, his translation has little to recommend it. Its advantage, however, is that it does take the reader from *The Shahnameh's* beginning to its end, but Levy had an almost unerring instinct for missing out the most interesting parts of the poem. The most recent, and easily the most attractive, verse translation of any part of the poem is Jerome Clinton's version of the Sohrab and Rostam story (1987).

Atkinson's and Champion's verse versions are in heroic couplets, the Warners' and Clinton's in blank verse. After some hesitation I have chosen blank verse as the medium for the translation which follows. My hesitation came from the fact that *The Shahnameh* in the original is written in couplets that correspond fairly closely in length to the English heroic couplet, which would therefore seem to be an obvious form to use for the translation of the poem. Another perhaps irrelevant but nevertheless beguiling consideration was the fact that out of all Western authors, Ferdowsi most often sounds like Racine. It is true that there are vast differences—the compactness and relentless focus of Racine are largely absent from Ferdowsi—but Ferdowsi's interest in anguished conflicts of duty and passion and his brilliant handling of the rhetorical tirade can feel extremely Racinian to a Western reader. It was tempting to imagine Sudabeh's or Afrasyab's speeches in some kind of English equivalent of the Racinian couplet. I was swayed, however, by the fact that the relatively little heroic verse there is in English is usually in blank verse and that the heroic couplet has, in this language, traditionally been reserved for romance, social comment or satire—it has become for us a homely and immediate, or comforting and charming, medium. Despite the great rhymed versions by Pope and Dryden of Homer and Virgil, attempts at the spaciousness and sublimity of epic have traditionally been made in blank verse, and it is perhaps worth remembering that blank verse was expressly invented—by Surrey—for the translation of epic into English. (The numbering of the lines does not correspond to the Persian original text; it is simply intended to help the reader refer to parts of the poem more easily The subheadings were probably inserted by early copyists and not by Ferdowsi, which may explain why they do not appear consistently throughout the text.)

In preparing this translation my main authority has been the recent edition of the text of the story edited by Mojtaba Minovi (Tehran, 1984); I have also on occasion consulted the Moscow edition of the complete poem (eds. Bertel's *et al.,* Moscow, 1966–71) and Mohl's edition (reprinted Paris, 1976). My translation was unfortunately completed before I was able to consult the new edition of the Seyavash portion of the text edited by Khaleghi-Motlagh. Of previous translations I have found the most useful to be Mohl's, followed by that of George and Edmond Warner, though the texts used by both often differ considerably from recent recensions. I have also at times had reference to the Arabic translation of the poem by Bondari. As this translation precedes by over a hundred years all extant Persian language manuscripts of the poem and seems to be based on a very conservative text, it has often been used by scholars as an arbiter between rival versions in Persian manuscripts. I am indebted to Dr. Michael Zwettler, Associate Professor of Arabic at Ohio State University, for his patient explication to me of various points of Bondari's text. Scholarly and reference works which have particularly helped me include articles, chapters and books on *The Shahnameh* by Khaleghi-Motlagh, Ehsan Yarshater, Zabihollah Safa, Eslami-Nodushan, Shahrokh Meskoob, F. M. Javanshir, William Hanaway and Jerome Clinton. I have used the standard dictionaries, together with Fritz Wolff's *Glossar zu Firdosis*

Schahnameh, and I am particularly indebted to Nushin's '*Vazheh Namak*' (Glossary of rare words) to *The Shahnameh.*

I would like to thank my friends and colleagues; who have provided encouragement and criticism. My chief and overwhelming debt is expressed in the dedication of this translation to my wife and to our children.

LIST OF CHARACTERS

Characters in roman type take part in the story; those in italics an mentioned in the course of the story but are already dead when it opens.

Whereas in English the stress usually falls on the penultimate syllable of a name, in Persian it tends to be evenly distributed between the syllables and this may, to an English ear, sound as if it falls on the last syllable. In fact, a compensatory stress on the last syllable will probably bring the reader closer to a Persian pronunciation. For the purposes of the verse I have in general scanned the names as if the last syllable were stressed. There are two distinct 'a' sounds in Persian, a long sound as in 'father' and a short sound as in 'cat'. I have not indicated this distinction in the text as it would probably have proved distracting, but interested readers will find it marked below: 'a' is as in 'cat', 'a' is as in 'father'. The sound transliterated as 'i' is a long vowel, like the second vowel in 'police' or the vowel in 'seen'; 'gh' as in 'Aghriras' (and also 'q' as in 'Qobad' and in some place-names, e.g. 'Qajqarbashi') is, approximately, a very guttural hard 'g'; 'kh' as in 'Khosrow' is similar to the German 'ch' as in 'Bach', or the Scottish pronunciation of the final sound in 'loch'.

Readers who are familiar with the story may find some of the transliterations unusual; the two most notable are those of the name of the hero himself, and of the name of his queen, the daughter of Afrasyab. Seyavash has in the past been transliterated as 'Siyavosh' 'Siavosh', 'Siavash' and 'Siyavash'. The 'a' sound for the last syllable rather than the 'o' has been favored recently as the more correct; I have transliterated the first vowel as 'e' rather than 'i' because 'i' is reserved for a long vowel and it is indisputably clear from the poem's scansion that the name begins with a short vowel. Afrasyab's daughter is often called 'Farangis'; 'Farigis' is however the correct form.

Afrasyab: king of Turan; son of Pashang; father of Farigis; brother of Garsivaz and Aghriras.

Aghriras: son of Pashang; brother of Afrasyab and Garsivaz; killed by Afrasyab in a dispute over prisoners of war.

Andariman: warrior of Turan.

Arash: king allied to Kavus; nothing is known of him beyond this single brief appearance.

Bahram: warrior of Iran; companion of Seyavash.

Barman: warrior of Turan.

Borzin: warrior of Iran.

Damur: warrior of Turan.

Fariborz: warrior of Iran; son of king Kavus.

Faridun: former Iranian king; the fifth king of the world in the *Shahnameh;* father of Iraj, Salm and Tur.

Farigis: daughter of Afrasyab; second wife of Seyavash; mother of Khosrow.

Farshidvard: warrior of Turan.

Forud: son of Seyavash and Jarireh.

Garsivaz: leader of the army of Turan; son of Pashang; brother of Afrasyab and Aghriras.

Gerui: warrior of Turan; son of Zereh.

Giv: warrior of Iran; son of Gudarz.

Golbad: warrior of Turan.

Golshahr: wife of Piran; mother of Jarireh.

Gorgin: warrior of Iran.

Gudarz: warrior of Iran; father of Giv.

Harzebad: keeper of Kavus's harem.

Human: warrior of Turan.

Hushang: former king of Iran; the second king of the world in the *Shahnameh.*

Iraj: former king of Iran; son of king Faridun; killed by his brothers Tur and Salm.

Jahan: warrior of Turan; son of Pulad.

Jamshid: former king of Iran; the third king of the world in the *Shahnameh.* A great legendary figure who introduced the arts of civilization to mankind and vied with God; a Persian Prometheus.

Jarireh: daughter of Piran; first wife of Seyavash; mother of Forud.

Kaveh: blacksmith who led a populist revolt against the demon king Zahhak.

Kavus: Iranian king; son of Qobad; father of Seyavash and of Fariborz; husband of Sudabeh.

Kherrad: warrior of Iran.

Khosrow: son of Seyavash and Farigis.

Lahhak: warrior of Turan.

Manuchehr: former Iranian king; grandson of Iraj; father of Nozar.

Nastihan: warrior of Turan.

Nozar: Iranian king killed by Afrasyab; son of Manuchehr; father of Tus.

Pashang: former king of Turan; father of Afrasyab, Aghriras and Garsivaz.

Pashin: king allied to king Kavus; nothing is known of him beyond this single brief appearance.

Pilsom: warrior of Turan; brother of Piran.

Piran: chief minister of Afrasyab; father of Jarireh and of Ruin; husband of Golshahr; brother of Pilsom.

Pulad: warrior of Turan; father of Jahan.

Qobad: former Iranian king; restorer of the nations fortunes; father of Kavus.

Rostam: champion of the Persian army; friend and guide of Seyavash; brother of Zavareh.

Ruin: warrior of Turan; son of Piran.

Salm: son of king Faridun; murderer, with his brother Tur, of their brother Iraj.

Sepahram: warrior of Turan.

Seyavash: prince of Iran; son of king Kavus; husband of Jarireh and father of Forud; husband of Farigis and father of Khosrow.

Shavran: warrior of Iran; father of Zangeh.

Shideh: warrior of Turan; son of Afrasyab.

Sudabeh: daughter of the king of Hamaveran, chief queen of king Kavus, stepmother of Seyavash.

Tovorg: warrior of Turan.

Tur: son of king Faridun; founder of the land of Turan; murderer, with his brother Salm, of their brother Iraj.

Tus: warrior of Iran; confidant of Kavus; son of Nozar.

Zahhak: demon-king of Iran, defeated by Faridun

Zal: father of Rostam, king of Sistan/Zabolestan.

Zangeh: warrior of Iran, companion of Seyavash; son of Shavran.

Zavareh: warrior of Iran; brother of Rostam.

Zereh: warrior of Turan; father of Gerui.

THE LEGEND OF SEYAVASH

And now, o expert story-teller, make
A well-turned narrative for us; whenever
A poet's words conform to wisdom's ways
His spirit brings us comfort (while the man
Whose thoughts are ugly finds his purposes
Spoilt by that ugliness, he crucifies
Himself and is a laughing-stock to those
Who understand; though no man sees his own faults,
You think your character's all spotless brilliance!)
But, if a work's to last, first make it well   10
And then you must present it to the learned;
If they approve, it's passed the test and on
It flows like water in the stream you've made.
Now make a story from the words the lord
Who gathered ancient legends[1] has passed on,
See you recite the matter faithfully.

These stories have grown old, but now, through me,
They'll live again, renewed, among the people—
And if a long life's granted me, if I'm
To stay a while here in life's pleasant vineyard,   20
A fruit-tree will remain when I am gone,
Displaying splendid fruit above the meadows.
A man who's lived to fifty-eight like me
Has seen innumerable wonders happen,
But his ambition stays as strong as ever,
And still he combs through almanacs or has
His fortune told to know what's going to be.
But wise men say, What's old cannot grow young.'
In all your eloquence be circumspect,

30   Seek fame throughout the world, and when you've gone
        It's God who will decide if hell or heaven
        Awaits you. But remember, as you sow
        So shall you reap, and what you say will be
        The words you'll hear men speak of you; the man
        Who's gently spoken never hears harsh words—
        Seek only justice in the world. Return
        Now to the story which that lord collected;
        Watch for the words the poet will recite.

THE BEGINNING OF THE STORY

        A priest of Zoroaster[2] said: One day,
        At cock-crow, Tus and Giv, Gudarz's son,
        Accompanied by a group of horsemen, left
        Their king's court in good spirits to hunt wild asses
        With hawks and cheetahs on the plain of Dagui.
        They killed enough to last for forty days.
        They weren't that far from Turkish territory—
        The land was black with Turkish tents—when in
        The distance, near the border with Turan[3]
10   They saw a thicket; Tus and Giv rode on,
        A few retainers following them; the two
        Approached the place and circled it,
        And, hidden in the bushes, there they found
        A beautiful young girl; both laughed aloud
        And hurried forward, for in all the world
        She had no equal, in her loveliness
        There was no fault. Giv spoke to her, 'You are
        As heart-bewitching as the moon, how have
        You made your way to this dense thicket here?'
20   She said, 'Last night my father set on me—
        I ran away from home. He'd come back late,
        The night was dark and he was tipsy from
        Some marriage-feast; when he caught sight of me
        While he was still a long way off, he drew
        His glittering dagger, threatening that he'd hack

My head off from my body there and then.'
The warrior asked her next about her lineage;
She answered him precisely, 'I am from
The family of Garsivaz, we trace
Our line back to king Faridun himself.'⁴ 30
'But how' he urged, 'did you get here on foot,
Without a horse or guide?' She said, 'My horse
Collapsed, exhausted, under me; I'd brought
A quantity of gold and jewels, and I'd
A gold crown on my head—men robbed me on
That hill-top over there, they beat me with
The scabbard of a sword. And when my father
Discovers what has happened he is certain
To send his horsemen chasing after me,
My mother too is sure to hurry here— 40
She wouldn't want me to desert my homeland.'
The warriors' hearts were softened by her words,
But Tus the son of Nozar lost all shame
And said, 'I found her, since I got here first—
She's mine.' Giv answered him, 'My noble lord,
Weren't you with me and all the rest of us?'
But Tus snapped, 'My horse got here first!' Giv said,
'Don't talk such rubbish! My horse led the field—
Don't stoop to lying for a slave-girl; a man 50
Who's chivalrous is never quarrelsome.'
Their argument grew so intense that they
Were ready to decapitate the girl;
Their angry wrangling only ended when
A warrior interposed, suggesting that
They take her to the king and there they both
Abide by his decision on the case.
Neither objected and they turned back to
The Persian court. But when Kavus beheld
The young girl's face he laughed, then gnawed his lip;
He said to both the warriors, 'Well, I see 60
You've lightened your long expedition's trials!
Now we can pass the day recounting how
Our warriors catch the sun with hunting cheetahs;

She is a deer, a beautiful young doe,.
Such prey is worthy of the best there is!'
He asked her then, 'What family are you from?—
Because your face seems like an angel's face.'
She said, 'My mother's from Khatun, and on
My father's side we trace our lineage back
To Faridun. My father's father is
The great commander Garsivaz, and in
The border marches his tent's at the centre
Of our encampment.' King Kavus replied,
'And you were ready to abandon to
The winds this face, this hair, this family?
You're worthy of a gold throne in my harem,
I'll make you first among the women there.'
She said, 'I saw you, and before all others
I chose you for my own, my lord.' The king
Dispatched this lovely idol to his quarters
And ordered that they seat her on a throne;
There she was dressed in cloth of gold, arrayed
With rubies, turquoise, lapis-lazuli,
And given every gift her state deserved;
She was herself a ruby, pure, uncut.

Then, some time later, when the world put on
Spring's vivid colors, she gave birth to a child
Angelic in his beauty, with a face
As lovely as an idol carved by Azar.[5]
They told Kavus, 'From your encounter with
That bright auspicious moon, a splendid child
Has come—your throne should touch the clouds for joy!'
The world was filled with talk about this wonder—
No man had ever heard of such a face,
Such hair . . . the world's king named him Seyavash
And had his horoscope worked out by one
Who knew the heavens and which conjunctions meant
Good fortune, which signalled a malignant fate.
He saw the infant's stars were inauspicious,
That Fortune would not smile on him; the king

Grew pensive; good and bad foretold a life
Of pain—he prayed that God would be his refuge.
Then Rostam, the renowned, of mammoth strength,
Came to the court. 'It's I,' he said, 'who must
Bring up this lion-like baby in my arms:
None of your entourage are capable
Of looking after him—in all the world
There's not a better nurse for him than me!'
For a while the king considered his suggestion,
And since the thought of it was not a weight   110
Within his heart he gave his heart's desire,
The apple of his eye, this perfect princeling
Into Rostam's arms. The warrior took the boy
Back to Zavolestan, his homeland, where
He built a lodging for him in an orchard.
He taught him horsemanship, the management
Of bridle, stirrup, bow and lariat;[6]
All that pertains to riding; how to sit
In council; how to drink appropriately;
The use of hawks and falcons, how to hunt;   120
What justice and injustice are; the duties
Attendant on the throne and crown; how to
Harangue his troops and lead them out to war.
He taught him every skill, from end to end,
And all the trouble Rostam took bore fruit—
Prince Seyavash became a paragon
Unmatched by any noble in the world.
Time passed and Seyavash grew tall, a man
Who hunted lions with his lariat;
He said to noble Rostam, 'How I long   130
To see the king! You've taken so much trouble,
Endured such heartache passing on the skills
A prince must know, my father ought to see
In me the outcome of great Rostam's teaching!'
The lion-hearted warrior began
His preparations for the prince's journey;
He sent out envoys to amass slaves, horses,
Gold, silver, seal-rings, thrones, crowns, belts, clothes, carpets—

From every quarter he had goods collected;
140 Whatever wasn't in his treasury
He quickly scoured the world for, and had brought.
With all this he equipped prince Seyavash,
Since everyone would watch him as he travelled,
And he himself escorted him, so that
The king would have no cause to take offence.
The people wished him well and filled the world
With splendor in his honour, mixing gold-dust
With ambergris and from triumphal arches
Sprinkling the mixture on the prince's head;
150 The world was given over to rejoicing
And decorations covered every house's
Roof and doorway; the horses trod on coins,
Their manes were smeared with saffron, wine and musk—
In all Iran there was not one sad soul.

When news reached king Kavus that Seyavash
Was coming home in glory, he sent out Tus
And Giv together with escorting troops
To welcome him with kettledrums and trumpets.
Then all the nobles gathered, men like Kherrad,
160 The conqueror of armies, and like Gorgin,
And went out in a body to receive
The righteous Seyavash. A shout went up
As soon as the assembled warriors saw
The king's son, and they cleared a path for him.
Three hundred slaves with censers of sweet smoke
Stood reverently around him; countless jewels
And golden coins were scattered where he walked.
From every side came cries of praise and homage.
When Seyavash saw king Kavus in state
170 Upon his ivory throne, the crown of rubies
Glittering on his head, he first bowed down and made
A deep obeisance, whispering secrets to
The earth a while, and then approached the king
Who took the youth's head in his hands and stared
In wonder at him, calling down God's grace

On one of tender years who showed such wisdom,
As though his spirit had been tutored by
The Spirit of Discretion. The king gave praise
To God repeatedly, bending his face
Down to the ground in prayer and said, 'O Thou   180
Who didst create the heavens, O Lord of light
And wisdom, all benefits on earth derive
From Thee, but first I praise Thee for my son.'
Then, questioning the boy concerning Rostam
And making much of him, he sat him on
A turquoise throne. The nobles of Iran
Came forward eagerly with presents for
The prince—they were astonished by his glory
And called down blessings on his head from God.
The king commanded that the Persian troops   190
Parade before the prince, prepared for battle.
Throughout the palace, in the royal gardens
And in the great square, all the world rejoiced—
On every side festivities began.
Men called for entertainers, wine and music;
Kavus gave orders for a celebration
Finer than any prince had ever held.
The revels went on for a week, and on
The eighth day king Kavus threw open his
Great treasury's doors and gave to Seyavash   200
All kinds of gifts—thrones, crowns, swords, signet-rings
And Arab horses saddled with the skin
Of leopards, armor both for warriors
And their mounts, cash and purses filled with coins,
Brocade and jewels and every sort of wealth;
All this, but not the royal crown—the boy
Was still too young—its time was yet to come,
Though many promises of benefits
The future'd bring were given him. And so
The eighth year came and king Kavus commanded   210
That he be given the golden crown and belt
Of lordship over Khorasan; as was
The royal custom then the charter was

Inscribed on silk; the king conferred the lands
Called Kuhestan[7] on him since he was now
Grown worthy of the royal throne and greatness.

And then, one day, the lovely Sudabeh
By chance caught sight of Seyavash's face—
Her heart beat faster and she fell to brooding,
220   Melting like ice before a fire, worn thin
As is a thread of silk. She sent an envoy,
Saying to her, 'Tell Seyavash in secret,
"If you should suddenly appear inside
The royal harem, no one would object!" '
The envoy went and gave the prince her message;
His honour was affronted—indignantly
He answered her, 'I'm not a man for harems;
I won't take part in plots and subterfuges.'
Next day as soon as dawn broke Sudabeh
230   Came quickly to the king and said, 'My lord
Who rules our armies and whose like the sun
And moon have never seen, whose son's a man
Unparalleled on earth, and may the world
Rejoice in him! Dispatch him to your harem,
Your private quarters, where his sisters are—
The love these veiled girls feel for him has made
Their faces bright with blushes, wet with tears—
Then they can honour him and bring him gifts,
And make the tree of loyalty bear fruit.'
240   The king replied, 'An excellent suggestion!
Your love is like a hundred mothers' love.'
He called for Seyavash and said, 'Blood's thicker,
Boy, than water! You've sisters here in purdah
And Sudabeh is like your loving mother.
God's made you such that anyone who sees
You loves you, but what use are distant glimpses
Especially to those who are your kin?
Go to my harem, see the girls who live there,
Stay with them for a while and let them show
250   Their loyalty to you.' When Seyavash

Had heard the king he stared at him, dumbfounded,
Debating for a while within himself
How he could clear the dust that dimmed his heart,
Believing that his father sought to test him
(Kavus was highly knowledgeable, glib,
Suspicious, wary, always on the watch).
He writhed with inward pain, attempting to
Foresee the outcome of all this, and thought,
'If I go in his harem, Sudabeh   260
Will badger me.' His answer was as follows,
'The king conferred the throne and crown on me
Just as the sun illuminates the dust;[8]
No king as good and true, as wise and grave
As you has ever worn the crown; send me
To priests, to nobles, to experienced sages,
Or have me learn the handling of a lance,
Or mace, or how to bend a bow against
My serried enemies; or how to rule—
Court etiquette, the conduct of a banquet   270
With music, wine and stewards. But in
The harem of the king what can I learn?
Since when have women shown the way to wisdom?
Though if the king commands me I shall go.'
The king replied, 'Good luck to you, my boy,
May wisdom always be your life's foundation—
I've heard few speeches so well put, and if
You follow what you say your mind will prosper.
But here you needn't harbour such suspicions;
Enjoy yourself for once, don't be so gloomy—   280
Just look in on the girls and give them all
A little pleasure; it's your loving sisters
Who live in purdah there, and Sudabeh
Who's like a mother to you.' Seyavash
Replied, 'I'll come at dawn to carry out
Whatever it may be the king commands.'

There was a man whose name was Harzebad,
Whose heart and mind were clear of every evil,

Who never left the private quarters of
The palace, and who kept the harem's keys.
290   The Persian king instructed this wise man,
'Tomorrow when the sun unsheathes its sword
Seek Seyavash out—see you listen to
His orders—and tell Sudabeh to have
A present ready, jewels and musk and perfumes,
And let the slave-girls and his sisters shower
The prince with saffron and bright emeralds.'
The sun rose up above the mountain ridge
And Seyavash appeared before the king;
He greeted him and made a deep obeisance;
300   Kavus conversed a while with him in private
And when they'd done he summoned Harzebad
And gave him suitable instructions, saying
To Seyavash, 'Go with him now, and see
That you prepare your heart for something new.'
The two went off lightheartedly, without
Suspicion, but when Harzebad drew back
The curtain from the entrance Seyavash
Felt fear, a strong presentiment of evil.
Then all the harem's occupants pressed forward,
310   Eager to celebrate his presence there;
On each side bowls stood, filled with musk and coins
And saffron; at his feet they scattered agates,
Emeralds and golden coins; the ground was spread
With Chinese silks sewn close with precious pearls,
And there was wine and music and the sound
Of singers' voices; every head was crowned
With jewels, the harem was arrayed as if
It were a paradise replete with wealth
And lovely girls. When Seyavash approached
320   The audience hall he saw a glittering throne
Studded with turquoise, draped with royal silks,
And there sat Sudabeh as lovely as
The moon, a paradise of tints and scents.
There she presided, shining like Canopus
Above the wastes of Yemen, and beneath

Her tall crown clustering curls fell like a noose
Of musk down to her feet. Head bowed, beside
Her, stood a maid who held her golden slippers.
As Seyavash came through the curtains folds
Queen Sudabeh descended from her throne   330
And quickly, gracefully, came forward. She bowed,
Then held him for a long time in her arms,
Kissing his eyes and cheeks repeatedly;
She could not tear her gaze from him and said,
'Each day, and for three watches of each night,
I praise God in a hundred ways for you;
There's no man who can boast a son like you,
The king himself has no one who's your equal.'
But Seyavash was well aware what all
This meant, that such affection was ungodly.   340
Since it was wrong for him to stay with her
He hurried over to his sisters who
Invoked God's blessings on the prince and sat
Him on a golden couch. He stayed with them
A while before returning to the king.
The harem buzzed with gossip: 'What a man,
The crown of courtesy!' . . . 'As if he were
Beyond humanity . . .' . . . 'His soul breathes wisdom . . .'
When Seyavash was in his father's presence
He said, 'I've seen what's hidden in your harem;   350
All good things that the world provides are yours,
And you've no reason to reproach your God;
In treasure, might and glory you outshine
King Faridun, king Jamshid, king Hushang.'
Kavus rejoiced at what he said and had
His audience chamber decorated for
A banquet cheerful as the spring's return—
Men gave themselves to wine, to harps and flutes,
And they forgot the sure decrees of Fate.

When night came and the day grew dark, Kavus   360
Went to his harem, sought out Sudabeh,
And said, 'No secrets from me now! Say what

You think of his behavior and his wisdom,
Our prince's stature and appearance—
Did he please you, is he wise? And would you say
He's better from report, or face to face?'
Queen Sudabeh replied, 'The sun and moon
Have never seen your like upon the throne;
Who is there in the world who's like your son?
And why should talk about this fact be hidden?'
The king replied, 'If he's to live until
He reaches manhood, then the evil eye
Must not come near him.'⁹ Sudabeh replied,
'If you agree with my advice, my dear,
I'll find a wife for him of his own blood,¹⁰
And not from one of our great clans, someone
Who'll bear a son for him who's able to
Preserve his name among the great. Now I
Have daughters who resemble you, who are
Your children and entirely of your race;
Or if he were to seek a daughter of
King Arash, or of king Pashin, they'd be
Delighted by the match.' The king replied,
'This is exactly what I want to happen—
The greatness of our name depends on it.'

At dawn the following day prince Seyavash
Came to the king and called down blessings on
The crown and throne. The court was cleared to let
Father and son chat privately together.
Kavus said, 'There's a secret wish I have:
I long for God Who rules the world to grant
That from your seed a prince should grow who will
Maintain my name in years to come; that just
As I have been renewed in having you,
So your heart will rejoice in seeing him.
I've learnt, from what astrologers have said,
Your horoscope predicts that from your loins
A prince will come who will preserve our name.¹¹
Now choose some noble girl—there's king Pashin,

Look in his harem, there are others in   400
The house of king Arash; look everywhere
Then make your choice.' The prince replied, 'I am
The servant of the king and bow my head
To his commands; whoever he should choose
Is suitable; the lord of all the world
Disposes of his slaves as he would wish.
But it's not right that Sudabeh should hear
Of this, she won't agree to it; it's best
That we should not consult her in this matter,
And I'm not going back to her apartments.'   410
The monarch laughed at Seyavash's words—
He had no inkling of the water hidden
Beneath the straw.[12] 'It's you who has to choose,
You needn't think of her—or anyone,'
He said, 'Though she speaks well of you and cares
About your welfare.' Seyavash seemed pleased
By what Kavus said; somewhat reassured
He praised the king, bowing before the throne.
But inwardly he fretted, sick at heart,
Alarmed by Sudabeh and all her schemes—   420
He knew all this was her idea and felt
The thought of her would make him burst with rage.

And so another night went by and heaven
Turned in its course above the darkened mountains.
Queen Sudabeh sat radiant on her throne
And placed a diadem of rubies wrought
With gold upon her head; she summoned all
Her girls[13] and motioned them to golden couches
And said to Harzebad, 'Go now and tell
This Seyavash that he must take the trouble   430
To visit us and show his cypress stature.'
When Harzebad revealed his mistress's message
The prince approached and saw her crowned, enthroned,
Her lovely girls standing arrayed before her
As if her palace were a paradise.
Then she descended from her throne, her hair

And face adorned with jewels, and came to him;
She sat him on a golden couch and stood
Before him like a servant girl, her arms
440 Crossed reverently. She showed the prince the girls
Arrayed there, each one like an uncut jewel,
And said to him, 'Look on my throne and glory
Now at these girls, each with her golden crown,
Each one of them a virgin from Taraz,[14]
Whom God has made of modesty and coyness;
Whichever of them pleases you, tell me,
And look more closely at her face and form.'
Prince Seyavash glanced quickly at the girls
But none of them dared catch his eye—they whispered
450 To each other, 'The moon itself would be
Ashamed to gaze at him.' Then one by one
They came before his throne, and inwardly
Each girl was speculating on her chance
Of being chosen by the prince. When they'd
Withdrawn, queen Sudabeh said, 'Why so silent,
And for so long? Why won't you tell me which
You want? Your face has an angelic glory
And anyone who sees you, even from
A distance, swoons with love and chooses you
460 Above all others. Look with discretion's eye
On all my lovely girls and see which one
Is worthy of you.' Seyavash stood speechless
And gave no answer. In purity of heart
He thought, 'Better I innocently mourn
Than take myself a wife from one who is
My enemy. Our nobles have recited
For me the history of Hamaveran,[15]
What he once did to Persia's king, how he
Humiliated all our warriors;
470 And Sudabeh's his daughter, full of guile,
Eager to strip our tribe, to extirpate
Us root and branch.[16] When Seyavash's lips
Stayed sealed the radiant Sudabeh removed
The veil that hid her face and said, 'If one

Should see the sun in splendor and the new moon,
It would be no surprise if he should look
With little interest on the moon; you have
The sun itself before you now. The man
Who sees me on my ivory throne, my crown
Of turquoise and bright rubies on my head—   480
What wonder if he disregards the moon
And thinks all other beings beneath contempt!
If we can come to an agreement now,
And if you'll set your mind at rest, not try
To wriggle out of it, I'll give you one
Of these young virgins here to stand before
You as your slave; now swear this oath to me—
Don't try to twist your head aside from what
I'm saying—that when the king must leave this world
You'll be there in his place, reminding me   490
Of him, that you'll not suffer any harm
To come to me and that you'll cherish me
As dearly as he did. I stand before
You now and look, I give you all my body,
The sweetness of my soul. Take anything
You want from me, I give it to you freely,
My head won't dodge the noose you bring for it.'
Tightly she clasped his head, tore at her clothes,[17]
All sense of shame and modesty forgotten.
Prince Seyavash's cheeks blushed like a rose,   500
His eyelashes were warm with tears and in
His heart he said, 'May God preserve me from
This devil's tricks, from treachery against
My father and from friendship with the Fiend!
If I speak coldly to this shameless slut,
Her heart will seethe, she'll be enraged and she'll
Contrive some secret sorcery to gull
The monarch of the world; it's better I
Talk gently, keep her pliable and loving.'
So Seyavash said, 'Who in all the world's   510
Your equal? You're lovely as the waning moon,
You deserve the king as consort, no one else;

But now, for me, your daughter is sufficient,
No other girl could be as suitable.
Agree to this, propose it to the king
And see what answer he returns to you.
I too will ask him for her hand and in
Your presence swear to think of no one else
Until she's grown as tall as I am now.[18]
520   As for this other matter, for the love
You feel for me because of my appearance—
It's God who in His glorious power has made
Me thus, my lovely queen; keep all this as
Our secret, don't tell anyone, and I
Intend to keep it hidden too. You are
The first of women and pre-eminent
Among our nobles, and from now on I
Shall think of you as if you were my mother.'
He spoke and gravely left the room, but in
530   Her heart his words produced a wild confusion.

When king Kavus next visited the harem
And Sudabeh caught sight of him she hurried
Forward, saying she had good news, and described
Her interview with Seyavash. She said,
'He came and looked all round my audience chamber
Where I had lined up all our black-eyed beauties—
There were so many lovely girls there that
It seemed the moon rained down the dew of love;
But no one pleased the prince except my daughter,
540   None of the other girls seemed worthy of him.'
The king was so delighted by these words
You'd say he held the moon within his arms.
He flung the treasury doors wide open, piled
Up presents for the prince—so many jewels,
Such cloth of gold and golden belts, crowns, rings,
Bracelets, torques and noble thrones—all kinds of goods
Were brought, so that the world seemed filled with wealth.
But Sudabeh watched in a daze, her mind
A mass of jostling schemes; she thought, 'If he

Won't do as I command him, he can rip   550
My body from my soul for all I care;
I'll use whatever means the world provides—
Open, hidden, good or evil—to trap him.
And if he still fights shy of me, I'll go
Before the king and publicly accuse him.'

She sat enthroned, adorned with royal earrings,
A jeweled crown on her head, and to her court
She summoned Seyavash. She talked with him
Of this and that, then said, 'The king's prepared
A treasure-trove for you the like of which   560
No man has ever seen—such crowns and thrones,
Immeasurable wealth of every kind,
You'd need two hundred elephants to shift it,
And in addition he will give my daughter.
Look at me now, my face, my head, my crown—
What possible excuse is there for you
To slight my love? Why do you twist away,
Evading all my body and my face?
Since first I saw you I'm your slave, I weep
In wretchedness and long for you; my pain   570
Has blotted out the light of day for me,
To me the sun is like a darkened cloud.
For seven years my tears and blood have stained
My cheeks for you—give me one moment now
Of secret happiness, grant me one day
Of youth again, and I'll provide you with
Far greater treasures than the king has given—
Such crowns and thrones and royal ornaments!
But if you turn your head away from me,
Hardening your heart against my love and longing,   580
Then I'll destroy you with Kavus the king—
His eyes will look on you with glowering hatred.'
But Seyavash said, 'God forbid that for
The sake of lust I fling faith to the winds,
Be treacherous to my father, so separate
Myself from manliness and wisdom's ways;

You are the consort of the king, the sun
That lights his court, and such a sin should be
Unthinkable for you.' Then Sudabeh
590   Leapt from her throne in rage, in hatred stretched
Her claws toward him, crying, 'I told you all
The secrets of my heart and little thought
What foulness lurked in yours; so like a fool
You want to shame me, do you, make me seem
An idiot before the wise?' She wrung
Her hands and ripped her clothes, and with her nails
She scored both cheeks; a wail went up from her
Apartments and the noise spilt from her chamber
Into the street; such lamentations sounded
600   Within the gardens and the palace halls
It seemed that resurrection day had come.

News reached the king's ears—he descended from
His golden throne and hurried to the harem.
He saw the face of Sudabeh all scratched,
The palace filled with gossip, and his heart
Contracted; he asked from everyone what had
Occurred, unconscious of this stony-hearted
Woman's tricks. Sudabeh sobbed in front of him,
Weeping and wailing, tearing her hair, and said,
610   'This Seyavash came to my throne—he clasped
Me tightly in his arms and cried, "It's you
Alone I've always longed for—listen, I
Must tell you how my heart and soul are filled
With love for you—how beautiful your face is,
O why are you so cold to me?" He knocked
The crown off from my musky hair—and look,
My clothes are torn across my breasts, my lord!'
The king was deeply troubled by her words;
Closely he questioned her, and in his heart
620   He said, 'If she has told the truth, if she's
Not looking for some ugly end in this,
Then Seyavash's head must be cut off—
And this must be the way the evil chain

Will be unlocked; what are the sage's words,
"In such a business lust is turned to blood"!'
He cleared the harem, told his wise and faithful
Advisors to withdraw; in solitude
He sat upon the throne and called them both,
Queen Sudabeh and Seyavash, before him.
Then, gently and judiciously, he said
To Seyavash, 'You didn't do this evil,   630
I did—and I'm suffering for my foolish words;
Why did I ever send you to the harem?
Now I must grieve and you must tell your tale.
Be truthful now, describe to me what's happened—
Show me the face of truth!' Then Seyavash
Recounted how he'd come there and how wild
With passion Sudabeh had been. But she
Broke in and said, 'This isn't true—of all
The girls here he was after me, my body,   640
And no one else. I told him all the king
Had given him in public and in private,
My daughter and the crown, the wealth and cash
And piled up treasure, and I said, "I'll add
As much again, give every kind of wealth
As dowry for my daughter," but he answered,
'What's wealth to me? And I don't want to see
Your daughter since it's only you I want—
Without you, wealth and people all mean nothing!"
He tried to force me, grasped me tightly in   650
His stony grip. I wouldn't yield to him;
He tore my hair then, scratched my cheeks, and, O
Dear lord of all the world, I bear within
My womb a baby sired by you, I felt
Such anguish it was near to being killed,
How dark and comfortless the world was then!'
The king said to himself, 'I cannot trust
What either of them say and this is not
A business to be hurried since distress
Numbs wisdom, lulling it to sleep; first I   660
Must gather evidence, and when my heart's

Calmed down then it'll be a better witness.
I have to see which of the two is guilty,
Which worthy of a drastic punishment.'
He sought a way to ferret out the truth
And sniffed at Seyavash's hands, his chest
And arms, his person, every part of him;
On Sudabeh he smelt the scent of wine,
Fine musk and rose water—but there was no
670 Such smell on Seyavash, no sign that he
Had touched her. King Kavus grew melancholy,
Despising Sudabeh and sick at heart,
And inwardly he said, 'She must be chopped
To pieces with a sharpened sword.' But then
He fell to thinking of Hamaveran,
And of the tumult, the indignant outcry,
That would ensue. And he remembered how,
When he had been a friendless prisoner there,
With no one from his tribe or kin to help,
680 This Sudabeh had served him night and day;
How silently she'd sympathized with him;[19]
And thirdly that her heart was full of kindness,
Thinking that this should cancel every sin;
And fourthly that he'd little children by her,
And in his soul he could not face the thought
Of their unhappiness. But Seyavash
Was guiltless and Kavus knew him to be
A man of principle. He said to him,
'Don't think about all this; follow the path
690 Of prudence, wisdom, knowledge. Tell no one
What has happened—this rumor must not spread.'

When Sudabeh had seen the king's heart grow
More cold to her, knowing she was disgraced
She sought a way to further her foul cause,
Replanting once again the tree of rancor.
There was a woman steeped in magic arts,
In spells and wiles, who was her confidante,
Heavy with pregnancy and near her time;

She sought this woman's help, described her secret
And then said, 'First swear that you'll support me!' 700
When she had sworn the queen heaped her with gifts
And went on, 'Mention this to no one else:
Prepare a drug that will abort your children,
Empty your belly and don't break my secret,
And these aborted babes will lend some credence
To my lying stories. I'll tell Kavus,
"These babes are mine, and murdered by that devil!"
I hope that this will settle Seyavash,
It's my last chance; but if you won't agree
The luster of my credit with the king 710
Will darken, I shall have to leave the court.'
The woman said, 'I am your slave; my head
Is bowed to your commands.' When dark night came
The woman drank a drug that made her cast
Her devil's brood, two babes that seemed as if
They were the offspring of a fiend—but what
Would you expect from children of a witch?
Then Sudabeh said to a servant, 'Bring
A golden dish here,' and she placed the devilish
Children in it; she hid the woman, screamed 720
And threw herself down headlong on her bed.
The cries that went up from her private quarters
Brought all the slave-girls waiting in the hall
Running to her side—they saw the two dead babies
Lying in the dish, and lamentations reached
The heavens from the palace. Their cries came to
The ears of king Kavus, who sprang up, trembling,
From his sleep—he made enquiries and they told
Him what had happened to his moon-faced queen.
That night he could not breathe in his distress, 730
And with the dawn he rose distraught and came
To see his Sudabeh stretched out, the harem
In an uproar, and the two dead babies flung
On one side in a golden dish. The queen
Began to weep and said, 'Behold this shining
Sun of yours—look at the evil he has done,

And like a fool you trusted him!' The king
Became uncertain in his heart—he left
And brooded for a while and to himself
740   He said, 'What remedy can I provide
For all of this? I can't ignore it now!'

Then king Kavus sought out astrologers
And, summoning them to court, welcomed each one
And sat him on a golden seat; he talked
Of Sudabeh, the war that he had fought
Once with Hamaveran, so that they'd know
What she had done and understand her conduct.
He talked at length about the babies, though
Some things he kept back. For a week they worked
750   With planispheres and astrolabes, and at last
Declared, 'Can wine be in a cup you've filled
With poison? These two belong to someone else
They're not the king's, this woman's not their mother,
Since if they'd been of royal race we would
Have found them easily with our instruments—
Their secret's not apparent in the heavens
Nor on the earth; take this for a wonder.' They gave
The king and his assembly evidence
That pointed to a scheming, impure woman.
760   Kavus kept his own counsel, saying nothing
To anyone, hiding his thoughts within.
A week passed and the world was filled with talk
Of sorcery. But Sudabeh cried out
For justice, saying to the king who rules
The world, 'I was my lord's most trusted friend,
And his companion in adversity
When he was driven from his throne; my heart
Is wrung with anguish for my murdered babies,
One instant to the next I hardly hope
770   To live.'[20] He said to her, 'Be quiet, woman—
Why do you babble such disgusting speeches?'
And then he ordered all the palace guards
To ransack the entire city, to turn

The houses upside down in their attempt
To find her evil confidante; they found
A clue close by—the veteran searchers soon
Caught up with her and haled the luckless woman
Through the streets, dragging her before the king.
Kindly he questioned her and held out hopes,
And made her promises for many days,   780
Then threatened torture and imprisonment,
But no confession came of this, she would
Not tell him what she knew. He gave his orders,
'Take her away, use every means and trick,
And if she still says nothing, saw her in half—
As is the royal custom in such cases.'
They took her from the court and threatened her
With hanging, with the sword and dungeons, but
The sorceress only said, 'I'm innocent,
What can I say before your noble lordships?'   7900
They told the king what she'd replied and added,
'But God alone knows what is hidden here.'
He ordered Sudabeh to come before him
And the astrologers repeated what
They'd said, 'Both babies are a witch's brood,
Sired by the devil!' But Sudabeh was ready
With her answer, 'They know this isn't true—
There's plenty they could say, but it's kept hidden
And they won't speak for fear of Seyavash.
A pride of lions trembles in terror before   800
That warrior of elephantine strength;
He has the might of eighty elephants
And if he wished could halt the Nile itself;
A hundred thousand serried soldiers flee
From him—shall I have strength to stand against him?
Must my two eyes weep tears of blood[21] for ever?
And what astrologer dare contradict
Prince Seyavash once he has had his say?
If you don't grieve for your dead little children,
Although they're yours as much as mine, if you   810
Believe such crazy gossip, I leave our quarrel

To be decided in the other world.'
She wept more water from her eyes than the sun
Draws from the Nile; Kavus, the leader of
His troops, was deeply moved and wept with her.
Then, sick at heart, he sent out Sudabeh,
Brooding on what he ought to do. He said,
'I'll secretly investigate this claim
And find what's lurking at the bottom of it.'
820 He summoned all the priesthood of the land
And spoke at length to them about his wife.
A priest replied, 'The king's distress will not
Stay hidden long; if you would know the truth
Of all these counter-claims, then you must act
And throw the stone that breaks the pot in pieces.
However dear his son might be to him,
The king's heart will be hurt by his suspicions,
And on the other hand you'll brood about
This daughter of Hamaveran's great king.
830 Since each has made such contradictory claims
One of the two of them must pass through fire—
High heaven's promised that in such a trial
No injury shall touch the innocent.'
The king called Sudabeh and Seyavash
And seated them before him to discuss
The matter; finally he said, 'My heart
And intellect will not trust either of you
Unless a fire discovers and disgraces
Whichever of you's guilty.' Then Sudabeh
840 Replied, 'I answer in all honesty—
I've shown the king my two aborted babies
And no one's known a greater wrong than this;
It's Seyavash who must establish that
He's done no harm, and that he's never tried
To ruin me.' And so the world's king turned
To his young son and said, What's your opinion
Of this business?' Then Seyavash replied,
'Compared with this charge hell's of no account—
If there's a mountain made of fire, I'll cross it;

It would be shameful to evade the challenge.'[22]   850

Kavus sat brooding on his son and on
The splendid Sudabeh and thought, 'If one
Of these two proves a good-for-nothing,
Who then will call me king? My son and wife
Are like my mind and brain to me, and which
Of them will turn out to be innocent?
It's best I cleanse my heart of all this filth
And take this course, heartbreaking though it is;
What did that eloquent commander say,
"If you're irresolute, don't play the king!'"   860
He told his minister to have a hundred
Caravans of camels brought in from the plain
And these were put to bringing wood and kindling
While all the people of Iran drew near
To watch. The red-haired dromedaries brought
The wood in with a will; two mountains of
Incalculable mass that could be seen
Two parasangs[23] away were built with it.
He longed to see the door of righteousness:
This was the means by which he sought the key   870
That would release him from disaster's hold—
(All our privations come from women's wiles,
And if you hear this story to the end
You'll see it's best that you believe this fact.)
They built the firewood into two huge hills
On the waste plain while all the people watched.
There was a passage left between the heaps
Such that with difficulty four armed men
Might ride abreast between them. Next, the king
Gave orders that a priest should have black oil   880
Poured on the wood; two hundred men then lit
And fanned the flames—the day seemed turned to night,
So much black smoke went billowing up at first,
But soon the flickering flames licked through the smoke
And all the earth glowed brighter than the heavens;
The world was filled with shouts and roaring fire,

The plain was scorched from end to end and all
Those watching wept to see the smiling face
Of Seyavash. He came before his father
890   Calmly, a golden helmet on his head
And dressed in white, his lips all smiles, his heart
All hope. His mount was black—a horse whose hooves
Sent dust up to the moon's sphere when it galloped—
And he had sprinkled camphor on himself,[24]
As if his white clothes were a corpse's shroud.
Dismounting from his horse he bowed down low
Before Kavus; he saw the king's face filled
With shame, and when the king addressed his son
He did so gently. Seyavash replied,
900   'No need to grieve that Fate has turned out thus.
This infamy fills all my mind and if
I'm innocent, the trial will rescue me,
And if I'm guilty of this sin, then God
Will not protect me now. But, by the power
Of God who gives all benefits, I'll feel
No heat at all from this huge hill of fire.'
A cry of lamentation rose then from
The city and the plain, the whole world grieved
At what Fate wrought; the sound of wailing reached
910   Queen Sudabeh who went up on the roof[25]
Above the king's great hall to watch the fire;
She hoped that evil would befall the prince—
Her heart seethed and she muttered to herself.
The whole world watched Kavus, all mouths were filled
With curses and all hearts with indignation.
Then Seyavash, unhesitating, turned
Towards the fire and urged his black horse forward;
From each side tongues of flame leapt out, his horse
And helmet disappeared, and on the plain
920   The crowd's eyes strained through desperate tears to see
If he would ride out from the blaze. Then they
Caught sight of him and what a shout went up—
'The young prince has escaped the flames!' If it
Were water that he'd ridden through, his clothes
Would be bone-dry and show no trace of dampness;

So freely did his horse and cloak emerge
They seemed as if refreshed by fragrant jasmine—
For when it is the holy will of God
Fire's breath is as innocuous as water.
Leaving the hill of fire he crossed the plain   930
And shouts rose from the town and desert waste;
The army's horsemen galloped out and filled
The ground before him with flung coins; peasants
And nobles shared in universal joy,
Passing the good news on to one another—
'The Lord has justified the innocent!'
But Sudabeh tore at her hair in rage
And wept and scored her cheeks. When Seyavash,
The guiltless, stood before his father, no trace
Of smoke, fire, dust or dirt was seen on him.   940
Then king Kavus dismounted from his horse—
And all his host dismounted after him;
Closely the king embraced prince Seyavash
And asked his pardon for this sinful act.
But Seyavash bowed down before his lord
And pressed his face against the ground, giving thanks
That he'd escaped the great fire's heat and that
His enemy's designs had been frustrated.
The king said, 'O my brave young warrior,
Bright-souled, of noble race, when such a one   950
As you is born—and from a virtuous mother—
He'll rule the world.' Then he returned in state
To the great hall of his palace where he sat
Enthroned and happy, placing the Kayanid[26] crown
On his head. Wine was brought, musicians summoned,
And all that Seyavash could wish was granted.
The drunken revels went on for three days,
The treasury door stood open wide, unlocked.

The fourth day dawned. Kavus sat on his throne
The great ox-headed mace[27] held in his hand;   960
In rage he summoned Sudabeh before him,
Repeating all their previous talk, then said,
'You're shameless and you've done sufficient harm,

Too often you've tormented my hurt heart;
It's you proposed this sinful act, and then
Betrayed my young son's soul, thrusting him into
The fire—all this you did by sorcery.
No pleas for mercy will avail you now;
Get out of here, prepare yourself for death,
970   You are not fit to live and hanging is
The only punishment for such a crime.'
But Sudabeh replied, 'O king, bring fire
Down on my head, and if in punishment for all
That I've endured, my head's to be cut off,
Give your commands and I submit. So the fire
Took no revenge on Seyavash—but let
Him tell the truth and cleanse the king's heart of
All doubt that this was through Zal's sorcery;[28]
So may the king not hate me in his heart!'
980   He said to her, 'Still at your tricks! And you're
Not hunchbacked yet with all the weight of your
Impertinence . . .?'[29] Then from the assembled Persians
The world's king asked, 'In answer to the sins
She's secretly committed, what shall I do?'
All made obeisance to the king and said,
'The punishment for this is that her soul
Be torn from her, that she should suffer for
Her evil deeds.' He gave his orders to
The executioner: 'Take her, hang her from
990   A gibbet in the public street and see
You show no mercy.' When everyone condemned
Queen Sudabeh, the women of the harem
Screamed in anguish and inwardly the king's
Heart filled with pain; he paled, and Seyavash
Addressed him thus, 'Do not torment your heart
With this affair. For my sake now forgive
Queen Sudabeh this sin; it may be she'll
Accept advice and walk in virtue's paths.'
And inwardly he thought, 'If Sudabeh's
1000 Destroyed now by the king, eventually
He will regret this act and in his grief

He'll see me as its cause.' The king had hoped
To find some means by which he could forgive
Past sins; he said to Seyavash, 'Well, I
Forgive her, since I see her drowned in tears.'[30]
Prince Seyavash then kissed his father's throne
And rose and left the room. All the harem flocked
To Sudabeh, and bowed down low before her.

Some time had passed; Kavus's heart grew warm
Again towards her. Once more he felt such love   1010
He could not tear his eyes from her dear face;
And once again she sought to trick the king
By stealthy means, according to her nature,
So that he'd be estranged from Seyavash.
Her hints made him suspicious but he talked
To none of his nobility about it.
In such affairs as these a man needs faith
And wisdom, justice, knowledge—so far as he's
God-fearing he'll attain his heart's desire.
Don't foolishly drink down the cup that Fate   1020
Has filled with poison, and because you're not
God's rival or the world's lord, curb your rage.
It is the custom of the turning heaven
To hide its face from you. A sage gave good
Advice once for a story just like ours—
'No love like that for blood relations,' and when
A man finds out he has a worthy son
He should divorce himself from love of women.

Once more the world's great king sank deep in love,
Then news came from his spies that Afrasyab,   1030
Turan's king, with a hundred thousand Turks,
Picked horsemen all, was menacing their borders,
And the land was filled with rumors. King Kavus
Was troubled and he turned his thoughts from feasting
Back to fighting, calling a council of
His loyal Persian subjects. To them he said,
'God did not make king Afrasyab of earth

And water, fire and air, like other men;
How often has he sworn his treaties with us
1040   And made such weighty promises of peace!
And now again he gathers warriors
About himself, assembles armies, ignores
His oath to us, the treaties that he's made.
Who should oppose him now but me? I'll turn
The brightness of his day to darkness, undo
The glory of his name throughout the world,
Or like a sudden bolt shot from a bow
He'll muster soldiers to attack Iran
And lay vast stretches of our country waste.'
1050   A priest replied, 'But what's an army for
If you yourself must be there in the field?
Why waste such wealth and leave the treasury doors
Wide open? Twice before[31] your recklessness
Has given this great throne to enemies;
This time choose some champion, worthy of warfare,
Able to prosecute revenge.' The king
Replied to them, 'But I see no one here
Who has the power or the ability
To fight with Afrasyab; no, I must go,
1060   Quick as a ship that cleaves the waves; now leave
And let me think this matter through.' Seyavash
Grew pensive hearing this, and like an adze
His thoughts were sharpened. In his heart he said,
'It's I who must conduct this war. Gently
I'll ask the king; if he consents, then God
Will set me free from Sudabeh and from
My father's doubts at one fell stroke. Besides,
If I can outwit such a host, this war
Will win me fame.' He came before Kavus,
1070   His sword-belt buckled on, and said to him,
'I'm of sufficient rank to lead our forces,
And when we fight against Turan's great king
I'll have his chiefs' heads humbled in the dust.'
(God's purposes in this were that the prince,
When evil Fortune turned its face against him

Through plots and stratagems of worthless men,
Should perish in the country of Turan.)
His father welcomed Seyavash's words,
Happy that he should bind his sword-belt on
For battle; he made much of him, conferred   1080
New dignities on him and said, 'My jewels,
My treasures, are all yours; and from the way
You're talked of in Iran it seems that all
The army's yours already.' Then he summoned
Rostam the warrior, the elephant-strong.
Wisely and well he talked with him and said,
'No mammoth matches you in strength, the wake
Of dust struck up by Rakhsh's[32] hooves outdoes
The Nile; you have no rival in the world
For skill, for silent knowledge, and you reared   1090
Prince Seyavash; the iron bands that guard
Deep mines of gems fly open at your touch.
Prince Seyavash has come, his sword-belt buckled,
A raging lion—he roars at me, eager
To fight with Afrasyab; go with him now,
Don't take your eyes off him: if you're alert
Untroubled sleep is mine, but if your watch
Relaxes it'll be my turn to worry.
Your sword and bow ensure the world's safe-keeping,
The moon, the heavens themselves do not surpass you!'   1110
The hero Rostam said, 'I am your slave,
Whatever you command me I will do;
My soul and refuge are prince Seyavash,
His head and crown to me are like the heavens.'
The king applauded when he heard him, saying,
'May wisdom ever be your soul's companion.'

To the din of fifes and kettledrums the hosts'
Commander, Tus, appeared and troops assembled
At the court. The king unlocked his treasury's doors,
Giving out swords and maces, headgear, belts,   1110
Helmets, armor, lances, shields. To Seyavash
He sent the key that kept the treasury

Where uncut cloth[33] was stored and said, 'My soul
And all my goods are yours, do with them as
You will.' He chose twelve thousand horsemen from
The famous fighters gathered there—from Pars
And Kuch, Baluchistan and fierce Gilan,
And from the deserts of Saruch; he chose
Twelve thousand infantry as well, shield-bearers
1120   Worthy of war. He summoned next all those
Born in Iran, whoever was brave, prudent,
Free-born, of Seyavash's age and stature—
Famous and warlike warriors, men like Bahram
And Zangeh, Shavran's son. The five chief priests
Of Persia raised the banner Kaveh'd fashioned[34]
And the king commanded that the whole host gather
Outside the palace on the plain. So crowded
Was the scene that you'd have said there was not room
For one more horse's hoof, and in the sky
1130   Stood Kaveh's banner like a glittering moon.
Quickly the king rode past his serried troops,
Reviewing them, and said, 'I wish you well,
My famous harbingers of victory;
May none but Fortune favor you, and may
The eyes of those who wish you ill be darkened;
God give you luck and health in setting out
And victory and joy when you return!'
Then kettledrums were strapped on elephants[35]
And as prince Seyavash bestrode his horse
1140   He ordered all his warriors to mount.
For one whole day Kavus accompanied
Their march, his two eyes filled with flowing tears;
At last the father and his son embraced,
Both weeping like a rain cloud in the spring—
Their eyes wept desperate tears, each wailed aloud,
And, as they parted, in his heart each felt
He would not see the other after this;
Such is the custom of the turning heavens
That gives to man now sweetness and now poison.
1150   Kavus turned back towards the court; the prince

Went onward with his men, keen for the fray,
And took the army to Zabolestan,[36]
Where Rostam led them to his father Zal.
Here Seyavash was entertained a while
By Zal the hero, Fortune's favorite,
With wine and music—drinking now with Rostam,
Chatting with Zavareh, rejoicing on
Zal's throne, out hunting, in the palace harem.[37]
A month passed, and he led the army out
With Rostam's help while Zal remained behind.   1160
From Zabul they pressed onward into Kabul
And northern India, levying soldiers
From every quarter as they went, until
They reached Herat where many troops were raised—
In charge of them the prince put Zangeh, the son
Of Shavran. They marched to Talqan and Marvrud
With heaven as it seemed still smiling on them,
Then drew near Balkh and injured no one, not
So much as by a single unkind word.

And on the other side Barman and Garsivaz   1170
Led out their army like a mighty wind—
Barman was in the van and Sepahram
Accompanied him. News of the army's new
Commander came, 'An army's on the march
From Persia and a young prince leads the host;
Rostam accompanies him, the champion
Whose strength is as an elephant's.' Garsivaz
Dispatched a messenger to Afrasyab,
Quick as a skiff that skims the water, saying,
'A huge force is approaching from Iran,   1180
They're led by Seyavash and with him come
Great warriors like Rostam, whose huge strength
Is as an elephant's, whose one hand holds
A dagger and whose other holds a shroud.[38]
Muster your troops and don't delay, the wind's
Already in our sails, the ship plunges forward.'
As quick as fire the envoy reached the king

And there repeated what he had been told.

For his part Seyavash did not hold back,
1190   But like a raging wind pressed on to Balkh;
Now that his enemies were threatened by
The forces of Iran they felt that they
Could not delay until they heard their king's
Reaction, and Garsivaz the warrior saw
They had no choice but to prepare for battle.
And so, hemmed in by Persia's troops, he fought
Before the gates of Balkh; in three days two
Great battles were decided—then Seyavash,
Whose splendor animated all his men
1200   Sent infantry against the city's gates;
His mighty army poured in after them
And Sepahram and all his army fled
Beyond the Oxus, back to Afrasyab.

When Seyavash together with his troops
Had entered Balkh he ordered that a letter
Be written to his king with ink made up
Of musk, attar of roses and sweet spices,
Inscribed as was most fitting on pure silk;
'All praise,' he started, 'be to God, sole source
1210   Of victory and fortune, Lord of the sun
And of the circling moon, Who raises up
Men's crowns and thrones and diadems—whomsoever
He wishes He exalts, while to another
He brings lamentation and adversity—
In Whose commands there's neither "why" nor "wherefore",
To Whom as guide our wisdom must submit.
Now from this Lord Who made the world
And all that is therein, invisible
And visible, be blessings on the king,
1220   And may his every venture turn out well.
I came to Balkh in joy and triumph by the grace
Of him who holds the crown and throne
Of all the world; three days the battle lasted,

And on the fourth God gave us victory.
Barman and Sepahram have fled, like bolts
Shot from a bow, to Termez; my army now
Controls the land from here up to the Oxus,
The glory of my helm subdues the world.
King Afrasyab still bides his time in Soghdia,
Captain and host encamped beyond the river—   1230
And if the king commands, I'll lead our men
Across to wage war on the other side.'

When this description reached the king he felt
His crown and throne exalted to the sphere
Of Saturn; he prayed to God that this young tree,
The prince, should grow until he bore ripe fruit
And joyfully he wrote an answering letter
As sweetly fresh as spring that comes in April:
'May God Who made the sun and moon, Who holds
The world and Who bestows the crown and throne,   1240
Sustain your heart in happiness for ever
And keep it free from pain and all misfortune,
Rejoicing always in your victories,
Your glory, the casque of greatness and the crown
Of your nobility. You led our troops out,
Eager for war; fortune, skill and righteousness
Are yours and, though the smell of mother's milk
Still scents your mouth, your strength in battle snapped
The whippings on your bow. Now may your body
Keep its prowess always, and may your heart   1250
Attain to its desires. Since victory
Is yours you should delay a while; do not
Disband your troops but make good use of time
And fortify your camp, because this Turk[39]
Is like a devil, sly, of evil birth
And evil in himself, although he wears
A crown and has great power and thinks to lift
His head above the shining moon; don't be
In any hurry to continue fighting—
This Afrasyab will come to you to fight,   1260

And then if he brings his men to our side of
The Oxus stream, he'll drag his skirts through blood.'
He stamped the letter with his seal, called in
The messenger and, having given him
The missive, sent him on his way; the man
Rode over hills and valleys till he reached
The prince who, when he saw the letter from
Iran's great king, knelt down and kissed the ground
Rejoicing in his heart, forgetting all
1270   Anxieties; the words delighted him,
He laughed and touched the letter to his head,
Then carried out his sovereign's wise commands,
His heart unswerving in its loyalty.

And on the other side prince Garsivaz,
The lion-warrior, like wind-blown dust
Approached his king with bold and bitter words,
'The general Seyavash invested Balkh,
Rostam marshaled their men; mighty their army,
Made up of famous fighters, for every man
1280   We had they'd more than fifty infantry,
Proud bearers of the ox-head mace; like fire
Their footmen came with shields, and quivers filled
With arrows—the eagle does not fly like them;
They fought us sleeplessly three days and nights
Till our men's heads and horses drooped from fatigue,
But when on their side one of them grew weary
He stepped back nimbly from the fray, withdrew
And rested, then, refreshed, renewed the fight.'
King Afrasyab flared up like fire, 'What's all
1290   This babble about rest and sleep?' He glared
At Garsivaz as if he'd hack the man
In two, then yelled and drove him from the room
Rather than wildly vent his rage on him.
He gave commands, 'Call me a thousand lords,
Prepare festivities, fill all the steppe
With tents, let Soghdia shine with Chinese splendor!'
And thus he spent the day in celebration;

But when the sun that lights the world had sunk
From sight king Afrasyab abruptly sought
Rest, sleep, twisting and turning on his bed.   1300

When one watch of the darkness of the night
Was over Afrasyab cried out, as if
He were a man who spills his secrets while
Delirious, and trembled in his bed.
His slaves appeared, shouting, raising the alarm,
And when the news was brought to Garsivaz
That darkness dimmed the office of the throne
He ran to be beside his king and saw
Him sprawled out on the dusty floor. He clasped
Him in his arms, embracing him, and said,   1310
'Come, tell your brother what has happened here.'
The king replied, 'Don't ask, don't speak to me,
Give me a moment till my mind has cleared
And hold me tightly for a little while.'
As gradually this veteran of the world
Came back to consciousness, weeping and groaning,
They brought him torches and he clambered up
On his bed, still trembling like a wind-swept tree.
Then the ambitious Garsivaz questioned him,
'Open your lips, describe this wonder for us.'   1320
Great Afrasyab replied, 'No one has seen
Such things in dreams and I have never heard
From young or old that they have passed a night
Like this. I saw a desert in my dream
And it was full of snakes; the world lay deep
In dust and eagles thronged the sky. The ground
Was parched, as if the heavens had never smiled
On it with rain. To one side stood my tent,
Around it was an army of fierce warriors;
A dust-storm started blowing and overturned   1330
My banner; blood flowed freely, streaming down
From every side, and swept away my tent.
Then like a raging wind an armored host
Of horsemen from Iran attacked my throne—

What lances and what bows they bore! Each lance
Was spitted with a human head; they hurled
Me from my throne and hurried me along;
Desperately, hands bound, I looked from side to side
But there were none of my own people near.
A haughty champion dragged me headlong to
Kavus and there a throne stood shining like
The moon and on it sat Kavus's son;
At most he was fourteen, but when he saw
Me standing bound before him there his roar
Was like a thunder cloud's and with his sword
He split me to the waist; I screamed aloud
In pain—and with my cries and pain awoke.'
Then Garsivaz said, 'This dream of the king
Cannot but presage what his friends would wish;
Your heart's desires, your crown and throne, will flourish
And all your enemies be overthrown.[40]
We need a dream-interpreter, someone
Who's deeply versed in all such lore; we'll call
Clear-headed priests, astrologers, wise men,
Whoever knows about such things—men from
The royal court and from your lands at large.'

The crowd assembled at the royal court,
Anxious to know why they'd been summoned there.
The king then called them in and seated them
According to their rank and, having talked
With each of them of this and that, addressed
The famous sages thus, 'Pure-hearted men,
Auspicious, wise, if I hear talk about
This dream I've had, openly, covertly,
From anyone in the world, I will not leave
A single one of you who breathes of this
Affair alive, his head still on his body.'
To calm their fears he gave them gold and silver
In limitless amounts, and then described
His dream. But when the high priest heard his words
He was afraid and asked the king to give

1340

1350

1360

1370

Assurances of safety, 'Who could say
Correctly what this dream might mean unless
The king would make a promise to his slaves
And swear in all solemnity that we'll
Be treated justly by him when we say
What we can see The king then promised them
That they'd be safe and that he would impute
No sin to them. Their spokesman, who was wise
And eloquent, replied, 'The world-king's dream   1380
Means that a sleepless mighty army's come;
Led by a prince who's guided by experienced
Counselors. His king has sent him here because
His horoscope declares our country will
Be ruined by his onslaught. If our king
Opposes Seyavash, the world will turn
As crimson as brocade with blood and not
A Turk survive—the king will rue the day
He fought with him and, even if he kills
The prince, Turan will turn out leaderless,   1390
Without a crown or throne—from end to end
The land will fill with insurrections, war
And vengeance for the sake of Seyavash.
Then when your land lies waste, depopulated,
You will recall these truths. And if the king
Became a bird, he could not fly beyond
The heavens that turn above us; thus they turn,
Bestowing sometimes fury, sometimes love.'
When Afrasyab heard this he grew despondent,
Unwilling to wage war. He told these secrets   1400
To Garsivaz, rehearsed the mysteries
He'd heard at length and said, 'If I don't lead
My army against Seyavash, no one
Will come here for revenge and neither he
Nor I will die in battle; men will rest
From all this turbulence—Kavus will not
Seek vengeance and the borders of our land
Will not be filled with warfare; now, instead
Of battle and the quest for worldwide rule,

1410   I'll look for peace with former enemies
And nothing more. I'll send him gold and silver,
A crown and throne and countless jewels, and thus
I pray this harsh disaster threatening me
Will be averted—and if not, I fear
My soul will wither up and die. If I
Can sew the eyes of Fortune shut with gold,
It may be heaven will let me live in peace;
I only want from Fate what's written there
Since mortal men must live as God prescribes.'

1420   When heaven had turned through half its daily course,
The glowing sun displayed its face and all
The nobles crowded to the royal court,
Ready to give service, their diadems
Of office on their heads. The king convoked
A council of shrewd, tried and tested men
And said to them, 'The only gift that I
Have ever seen Fate offer me is war.
How many nobles from this great assembly
Have been destroyed in war because of me,
1430   How many towns are filled now with the sick,
How many gardens overgrown with briars,
How many orchards have I fought my way through!
My troops have left their traces everywhere—
And when the king of all the world's unjust
All forms of goodness hide themselves away:
On upland plains the wild ass casts her young
Too soon, the hawk's new squabs will grow up blind,
Milk dries up in the teats of animals,
The water in its courses turns to tar;
1440   Throughout the world streams fail and dry and in
The musk-deer's sac no scent of musk's produced;
As crooked dealing drives out righteousness,
Deceit and dearth spring up on every side.
But let us now remember wisdom, justice,
Let us bring justice now in sorrow's place
And may the world through us know peace—

Death must no longer take men unawares.
Since two thirds of the world are mine to rule
And both Iran and Turan are my home
I will, if you agree, dispatch a letter   1450
To Rostam, look for ways to make my peace
With Seyavash and send him countless gifts.'
Then, one by one, the nobles answered him,
All wanted righteousness and equity,
Saying, 'You are our king, we are as slaves,
Our hearts submit to all that you command.'

The counselors dispersed, their minds intent
On justice, none was troubled by the thought
Of grief or strife. To Garsivaz the king
Then said, 'Make preparations and be quick   1460
About it, hurry now, don't stop to chatter,
Select two hundred horsemen from the army;
Take costly fine-worked gifts of every kind
To Seyavash; take golden saddles set
On Arab horses, Indian swords in golden
Scabbards, a crown inlaid with royal jewels,
A hundred camel-loads of carpets—take
Two hundred slaves, young men and girls; tell him,
"We have no quarrel with you." Ply the prince
With countless courteous questions and then add,
"We've no designs against Iran, the land   1470
Up to the Oxus's banks is ours to rule;
I reign in Soghdia, which is a realm
Distinct from others and has been since the time
Of Tur and warlike Salm when all the world's
Affairs were rearranged, turned upside down—
And since Iraj's murder[41] wisdom's fled
The minds of our nobility; before
That time Turan was not divided from
Iran—and war and enmity were then   1480
Unknown. I hope that God will grant us peace,
Rejoicing, welcome news; He raised you from
Iran and looks with favor on your valor—

Through your good fortune all the world will be
At peace; evil and war will disappear.
Now Garsivaz has come to you to clear
The dark suspicions in your mind; let us
Divide the world as Faridun once did,
Bestowing it on his three valiant sons;
1490   Let us renew this wisdom, step back from
The brink of war, from battles for revenge.
You are a king yourself, speak to Iran's
Great king—it may be that his warlike heart
Will soften at your words." Talk too to Rostam,
That warrior of elephantine strength—
Flatter him fulsomely, tell him about
The slaves and horses with their golden trappings;
Take him such gifts as well (omit the throne
Of gold, he's not a king, a champion can't
1500   Be given such a royal gift), so that
This matter may be closed successfully.'

When Garsivaz had gathered all the gifts
And made the earth's face splendid with their glory
He quickly reached the Oxus's banks and chose
An envoy from his warriors to tell
The prince that Garsivaz approached his court.
It took a day to cross by boat[42] and then
He made his way impatiently to Balkh.
The messenger reached Seyavash's court
1510   And there announced, 'Prince Garsivaz approaches.'
Seyavash called Rostam to him and they talked
At length about this new development.
As Garsivaz drew near he ordered that
The way be cleared for him and when he saw
Him Seyavash stood up and, smiling broadly,
Made his excuses;[43] Garsivaz, while still
A long way off, bowed down and kissed the ground,
His face suffused with shame, his heart with fear.
Prince Seyavash allotted him a seat
1520   Below his throne, then questioned him at length

About king Afrasyab. As Garsivaz
Sat back and took in this new prince's crown
And court, he said to Rostam, 'When Afrasyab
Heard of your coming he immediately
Dispatched with me a trifling gift to give
To Seyavash.' He ordered that the presents
Be brought in and displayed to Seyavash;
Then from the city gates up to the court
The way was thronged with gold and horses, slaves
And diadems, and no one could compute   1530
The coins and crowns and mighty thrones, the youths
All with their ceremonial caps and belts,
The slave-girls with their golden necklaces
And bangles. Seyavash looked on, delighted;
His face was fresh and open as he heard
King Afrasyab's proposals. Rostam advised
His lord, 'First spend a week in feasting, then
We'll think of our reply; we must give thought
To this request and ask for all men's counsel.'
And when shrewd Garsivaz heard this he kissed   1540
The ground and made obeisance to the prince.
A house was fitted up for him with fine
Brocades, and stewards sent to serve his needs.
Rostam and Seyavash sat down to weigh
The complicated details of the case;
The hero Rostam was suspicious of
The fact that Garsivaz had come so quickly—
They had their scouts deployed in each direction
And took such measures as were necessary.
Then Seyavash asked Rostam, 'Why are they   1550
So anxious to make peace with us? Explain
This mystery—suggest an antidote
To neutralize their poison. But let's choose
A hundred of king Afrasyab's own kin
And have him send them here as hostages;
This would disperse the darkness of our doubts—
Since, God forbid, he might be desperate,
Beating his war-drums, out of fear, beneath

A blanket of pretended peace. This done,
1560   We must dispatch a loyal messenger
To tell Kavus of what we have decided;
It may be he'll give up his hopes for vengeance.'
Rostam replied, 'You've hit on it; this is
The only way we can conclude a treaty.'

When dawn came Garsivaz appeared at court,
Wearing his ceremonial belt and crown;
He kissed the ground in front of Seyavash
And greeted him respectfully. The prince
Addressed him thus, 'I've given long and hard
1570   Consideration to your words and actions
And we agree we want to wash all thought
Of vengeance from our hearts. Take this reply
To Afrasyab: "If secretly you're plotting
An attack on us, think that a man who sees
The evil ends of evil acts should turn
From evil doing; the heart that's radiant
With wisdom is a treasure filled with blessings.
If underneath your sweetness there's no poison,
If hidden in your heart there's no desire
1580   For hurt or harm, and if you are sincere
In wanting an agreement that we end
Our enmity and hatred, send me now
As hostages the warriors whom Rostam
Designates; next, you must evacuate
Whatever cities of Iran you hold,
Withdraw within the borders of Turan
And rest awhile from war and war's reprisals.
May there be only truth between us two
And I'll not bind my sword-belt on again
1590   Prepared for battle. I'll send a letter to
Kavus in hopes that he'll withdraw our forces." '
Immediately Garsivaz dispatched
An envoy, quick as a lion in pursuit,
Saying, 'Don't waste your time in sleep—go straight
To Afrasyab and tell him, "I've been quick

And diligent and all I sought I've gained,
But Seyavash needs hostages if you
Want him to give up his campaign against us." '

The messenger arrived and told the king
What Seyavash and noble Garsivaz   1600
Had said. When Afrasyab had taken in
Their words he writhed in agony and could
Not see his way ahead; he reasoned with
Himself, 'If I lose now a hundred of
My closest kin from this assembly, then
My whole court will disintegrate and there'll
Be no one left who's loyal to me; and if
I say, "Don't ask for hostages from me",
He'll think that everything I've said's a lie.
I'll have to send the hostages if this   1610
Affair depends on them for its success.'
He counted off a hundred of his kinsfolk
According to the list drawn up by Rostam,
Then sent them to the Persian prince and gave
Them splendid robes and many other gifts.
He ordered that the drums and trumpets sound;
The royal tent was struck and he withdrew
From Samarkand, Bokhara, Soghdia,
From Chaj and from the land and ivory throne
Of Sepijab, moving his men toward Gang   1620
Without deceit, excuses or delay.
When Rostam learnt of Afrasyab's retreat
His doubts were laid to rest; he hurried to
The prince as quick as wind-blown dust and said,
'The matter's turned out well and it is right
That Garsivaz return now.' Seyavash
Commanded that a robe of honour, armor,
A diadem and belt, an Arab horse
With golden harness and an Indian sword,
Its scabbard worked with gold, be given to   1630
Prince Garsivaz who, when he saw the robe,
Was so astonished that he seemed like someone

Who's seen the moon descend to earth; he left,
Praising prince Seyavash—it seemed his feet
Could hardly touch the ground in gratitude.

Then Seyavash sat on his ivory throne,
The ivory crown suspended on a chain
Above his head, and tried to think of someone
Whose language was persuasive, who could give
1640   The words he said the proper scent and color,
Some warrior from the army's cavalry
With whom Kavus was likely to get on.
Rostam, the hero blessed with mammoth strength,
Said to his prince, 'Who'd dare to broach the matter?
Kavus is still his old self—and his rage[44]
Is as it always was, not more nor less;
But I could go and tell the world's king what
He's not aware of yet. I'd split the earth
In two if you should order it, and I
1650   See only good as coming from my journey.'
The prince was overjoyed at his suggestion
And his anxieties about whom best
To send evaporated. He sat down
With Rostam to discuss the matter's details.

SEYAVASH'S LETTER TO KAVUS AND ROSTAM'S JOURNEY

He had a secretary called in to write
A letter to Kavus on silk. He began
With praise of God, from Whom he saw his strength,
His glory and his skill derive: 'Lord of
The intellect, of time and place, Who feeds
The wisdom in our souls, Whose orders none
Can countermand; the man neglectful of
The duty that he owes to Him sees loss
And sorrow in this world since He alone
10   Is Lord of wealth and righteousness. From Him
Be blessings on the king, master of the world,

Elect of all nobility, whose mind
Encompasses all good and evil, whose strength
And stature are a pillar of true wisdom.
I entered Balkh rejoicing in my Fate
As men rejoice in spring. When Afrasyab
Was given news of me the sun grew black
Before his eyes; he knew adversity
Had sought him out; Fortune no longer looked
With favor on him and his world was darkened.   20
His brother came with gifts and countless slaves,
All beautiful and richly dressed; he seeks
The king's safe-keeping and resigns to him
The crown, the royal throne; he will content
Himself with what he has within his borders,
Observe his station, give up all Iran's
Dark soil to us, completely cleanse his heart
Of thoughts of warfare and revenge.
He's sent as hostages a hundred of
His kin to me and Rostam comes to ask   30
The king to pardon him—as would be right
For one of your benevolence, whose face
Is witness to the kindly heart within.'
The letter written, warlike Rostam turned
His face toward Kavus's court and on
The other side the loyal Garsivaz
Approached king Afrasyab, commander of
The armies of Turan. He gave a full
Account of Seyavash and said, 'No king's
His equal—not in beauty or behavior,   40
In intellect, speech, kindness, modesty;
He's brave and eloquent, a horseman and
A warrior; you'd say that wisdom's home's
Within his heart!' Laughing, Afrasyab replied,
'A bit of policy beats fighting then,
My loyal brother!—besides, that dream alarmed me;
It seemed I was about to slip from power
And, filled with overwhelming fear, I looked
For cunning ways to ward off my decline—

50   And I've accomplished it with cash and treasure;
      It's all turned out exactly as I wished!'

      And on the other side the lion-warrior
      Great Rostam came to king Kavus, as quick
      As wind-blown dust, his arms across his chest
      In sign of his submission. The king rose from
      His throne, enfolded him in his embrace
      And asked for news of Seyavash his son,
      How Fortune treated them, of fighting men
      And battles, what the army had accomplished,
60   And why he had returned. First Rostam praised
      Prince Seyavash at length, then gave the king
      His letter. But when the chief scribe read it out
      The world-king's face grew black as pitch; he said
      To Rostam, 'I'm aware he's young and that
      He's no experience of such wickedness,
      But you—there's no one like you in the world
      For warfare, lion-warriors long to prove
      Themselves in combat man to man with you,
      And haven't you seen Afrasyab's great crimes
70   And how he's wrested me of food and sleep
      And all repose? I should have gone but I
      Held back, although my mind was filled with thoughts
      Of enmity for him. I didn't go
      Because they said, "Don't stir from here—stay here
      And let the young prince manage it." When what
      Was wanted was God's vengeance on this evil
      And condign punishment against his crimes;
      Your hearts are charmed by all the sickening wealth
      He's looted from the innocent and by
80   A hundred wretched misbegotten Turks—
      Low bastards who don't know their fathers' names—
      And when will Afrasyab consider them?
      In his eyes they're the filth that clogs the street.
      But if you've given up on wisdom, I'm
      Not tired yet of campaigns and war; I'll send
      A proper man to Seyavash, someone
      With sense and strategy, and I'll tell him,

"Raise a huge fire, fetter these low Turks' feet
With massive chains, and fling their wealth in the flames-
Don't keep a single jot of it; then send   90
These captives here to me because I mean
To chop the heads off from their bodies now.
Next, rouse yourself for war and lead our host
Without delay against his capital;
Unleash our men like wolves against a flock
Of sheep—if you can bring yourself to learn
His evil ways and have our army burn
And loot, this Afrasyab will fight you—when
His rest and sleep are ruined." ' Rostam replied,
'My lord, don't be alarmed by what's been done   100
But listen to my words: first you're our king
And then the whole world's under your command;
Your orders were, "Don't be in any hurry
To cross the Oxus looking for a fight
With Afrasyab; stay where you are and let
Him come to fight with you—because he's rash
And won't hold back." So we relaxed the pressure
Of our attacks—but from the first he opened
This door of peace. It isn't right to look for war
Against a man who's making overtures   110
Of peace, who thinks of holidays and banquets.
And for the king to break an oath will not
Be well received by those who wish him well.
Prince Seyavash has been victorious.
He fought this war like an unflinching leopard;
And what did you desire besides your throne
And crown, the seal-ring on your finger, your
Security, the treasure of the land
That is Iran? And you have gained all these!
Why wildly look for war? Don't wash your bright   120
And noble heart in muddied waters now.
Suppose that Afrasyab is secretly
Preparing to renege on all he's said,
Well, we're not tired of war—the lion's claws
And our sharp swords are still in place. Don't ask
Your son to break the oath he's made, don't do

What is unworthy of the crown; I must
Speak openly—prince Seyavash will not
Go back on what he's said, and what the king
130   Suggests will horrify that noble hero.'

Kavus heard Rostam's words and started up,
Enraged, his eyes dilated in his fury,
And said, 'So now you must speak openly!
It's you who's put these notions in his head,
Who's torn the roots of vengeance from his heart!
You looked to have an easy time of it,
Cared nothing for the glory of our crown
And throne and seal—well you stay here while Tus
The great commander straps the drums of war
140   On elephants to finish off this business.
I'll send a messenger to Balkh this minute.
He'll bear a letter filled with bitter words—
If Seyavash attempts to wriggle free
From loyalty to me, if he evades
My orders, he must give up his command
To Tus and come back here with all his henchmen—
If his mind's filled with disobedience,
He'll see from me the treatment he deserves.'
Then Rostam was enraged and said, 'The heavens
150   Themselves can't lord it over me; if you
Think Tus a better warrior than Rostam,
Then you should learn how rare such Rostams are!'
With that he left the king, beside himself
With rage, his face contorted in his anger.
Immediately the king called Tus and gave
Commands to have the army readied for
The road; Tus left the presence of his sovereign
And ordered kettledrums and bugles sounded.
The army was to march and by its battles
160   Bring all this business quickly to an end.
Meanwhile Kavus gave orders that an envoy
Be ready to set out to Seyavash.

KAVUS'S ANSWER TO SEYAVASH

He had a scribe called in, assigned the man
A gold-worked seat and started to dictate
A hostile, angry letter full of harsh
Expressions, bitter as a bitter lime.
He started, 'Praises be to the Creator,
The Lord of peace and war, of Mars, the moon
And Saturn, good and evil, glory, power—
It is by His command the heavens turn,
Through Him that light diffuses everywhere.
May health and Fortune and the crown and throne   10
Be ever yours, my boy, although my orders
Have been obscured within your heart and your head's
Grown thoughtless in the sleep of youth. You've heard
Of how Iran was dealt with by this foe,
When on the day of battle he gained victory:[45]
Don't foolishly expect his friendship now,
Don't strip our court of all its dignity
And, if you don't want Fate to bring you down,
Don't push your head—because of youthfulness—
Into his snare. How often I've turned back   20
From fighting him because of his glib lies!
It won't be anything remarkable
If he tricks you; he should be judged by how
He's treated me. I made no mention of
The possibility of peace with him,
You've turned your face away from what I ordered.
As for this Rostam, he can't get enough
Of wealth and treasure, and if your longing for
This wretched royal crown I wear has made
You wary of pursuing war, seek out   30
The way of independence with your sword;
It's conquered territory that gives a king
His standing. When the army's leader Tus
Arrives he'll take all your affairs in hand.
As for these hostages that you've got hold of,

Load them with heavy chains at once, set them
On donkeys—send the slaves, the gifts, the lot,
Immediately to court. And as for you,
Prepare for vengeance and for war, don't talk
40   About it needlessly, at length; attack
By night and make the dark earth flow with blood,
A second Oxus. Their commander won't
Be stopping for his sleep, this Afrasyab
Will come to fight against you. And if you
Feel pity for this devil, if you're afraid
They'll label you as one who breaks his word,
Then hand the army over to great Tus—
You're worthless as a warrior on the day
Of battle, only fit for pretty girls,
50   Preferring soft festivities to fighting.'
They closed the letter with the royal seal;
As if he'd sprouted winds the envoy sped
Along the road. When Seyavash received
The message and had seen its unkind language,
He called the envoy in and questioned him,
Had him go over all that had been said.
The man recounted what had happened to
Heroic Rostam, the affair of Tus,
Kavus's rage. When Seyavash had heard
60   His tale, he turned aside his face and grieved
For noble Rostam, brooding in his heart
On what his father'd done and on the Turks,
And on the day of battle. To himself
He said, 'A hundred Turkish cavalry,
Illustrious men, all kinsmen to their king,
All loyal, all innocent—if I should send
Them to Kavus, he won't inquire or care
About the things they've done, but there and then
He'll string them up alive; and what excuse
70   Can I then bring to God? The world's affairs
Have brought down evil on my head—and if
Now in my innocence I thoughtlessly

Wage war against the leader of Turan's
Great army, God Who rules the world will not
Take kindly to this evil from my hands,
The tongues of everyone will speak against me;
And if I give the army up to Tus
And go back to my king, from him too evil
Will descend on me—to left and right I see
No course but evil, and ahead too evil;   80
Nothing but evil's come from Sudabeh—
I have no knowledge of what God will bring.'
He called two warriors from the army—Bahram
And Zangeh, Shavran's son, who'd both been in
His confidence since Rostam left—then cleared
The court and had them sit in front of him.
He said to them, 'An evil destiny
Heaps evils on my head; the king's kind heart
Was like a noble tree, all leaves and fruit;
Since Sudabeh deceived him you could say   90
It's turned into a harsh corrosive poison;
His harem has become my prison cell,
My heart and happy Fortune changed to grief;
It was my adverse Fate that made her love
For me flare up in flames of lust and, cursed
By bitter Destiny, I looked for war—
A means to stay away from her fell claws.
Their army led by vengeful Garsivaz
Invested Balkh, king Afrasyab held back
In Soghdia with a hundred thousand swordsmen,   100
Brooding on revenge—and, like a mighty wind,
I went, sought no delay in war with them.
When they'd withdrawn entirely from this country
And sent the hostages and gifts, all our
Advisers were agreed we should turn back
From our campaign against them. But the king,
Displeased by what I've done, now looks for ways
To persecute me, to destroy my life.
Wildly he forces me to fight—I fear

110 He'll make me break the oath that I have sworn to.
If he wants wealth from war, now that he's got
Such treasures and our country in his grasp,
What point is there in wildly shedding blood,
In giving up our hearts to vengefulness—
Which must mean that our heads are turned aside
From God, that we'll be blamed by everyone?
He'll snatch both this world and the world to come
From me, I'll be as Ahriman[46] would want me.
I wish my mother'd never given birth
120 To me, or that in being born I'd died,
Since I must see so many sorrows, taste
Such poison from the world. This oath I've made,
This treaty that I've sworn to before God,
Are such that if I turn my head away
From righteousness calamities will come
From every side. The whole world knows that I've
Concluded peace talks with the Turkish king
And everyone in every place will say—
Deservedly—that I've done wrong. If I
130 Should cut myself from all religious scruples,
Go back to vengeance, twist my head aside
From heaven's and earth's proprieties, how can
The God who made the world approve of me
Or turning Fortune smile on me again?
I'll go, I'll search the world for some land where
My name will never come to king Kavus;
The brightness of my days will pass as He
Who orders all the world decides. The man
Whose head's devoid of intellect cannot
140 Distinguish good from bad; Qobad[47] came here
And reigned and died, relinquishing the world—
And this king too I have to count as dead.
Now Zangeh, Shavran's son, get ready to
Exert yourself, to travel to the court
Of Afrasyab; don't pause for rest or sleep,
Take all this treasure—cash, crowns, couches, thrones;
Together with the hostages, return

Them all and tell him of the quandary that
I'm faced with.' Then to Bahram, Gudarz's son,
He said, 'Command of this great army, of   150
The marches of our country, of the wealth,
And of the elephants that bear our drums,
I now resign to you till Tus arrives;
Deliver them to this great leader's hands,
See everything's arrayed in perfect order,
And one by one count out to him our treasures,
Couches, crowns, thrones.' When Bahram heard his words
His heart was wrung for Seyavash's pain
And Zangeh, Shavran's son, wept desperate tears—
Cursing the country of Hamaveran.[48]   160
The two sat sunk in grief, made heart-sick by
Their prince's words. They said, 'You can't mean this—
Without your father, there's no place for you
In all the world; compose a letter to
The king and ask for Rostam back again;
Now that the tree of greatness flourishes,
Don't bring disaster on our heads.' But he
Did not accept these two wise warrior's words,
High heaven's hidden course willed otherwise.
He answered them, 'The king's command for me   170
Is higher than the sun and moon, but nothing—
Not motes, not lions or elephants—can rise
Against God's will; the man who disobeys
His God has wandering wits, he's lost himself.
And must I now imbrue my hands with blood,
And lead two countries into wars of vengeance?
And who knows which side Fate will favor in
This battle? The business of the hostages
Infuriates my father, he'll repeat
What he's already said and I've refused;   180
He looks for rage and warfare once again
And all the tears of sorrow that come with them.
But if your hearts are troubled by my actions,
And if your minds rebel against my words,
I'll be the messenger myself and choose

Another captain to command this plain
Now filled with all our tents.' When Seyavash
Had answered in this way the souls of both
These haughty warriors withered and they wept
190   As if a fire consumed them at the prospect
Of their parting. The eye and heart of Fate
Were secretly against their prince—they'd not
See him again and this was why they wept
At his decision. Zangeh answered him,
'We are your slaves, our hearts are filled with love
For you, our general; may our souls and bodies
Find ways to sacrifice themselves for you,
And may our loyalty stay true till death.'
When he had heard his faithful friends' reply
200   The wary prince told Zangeh, 'Go, report
To Afrasyab, the lord of Turan's armies,
The way this business has turned out for me;
Say all my profit from this peace is discord,
The sweets are his, the pain and poison mine—
Say I won't wriggle out of what I've sworn,
Though it must mean I lose the royal throne;
The God who rules the world's my refuge,
The ground's my throne, the turning heavens my crown.
And further, since I've willfully not done
210   What king Kavus has ordered, I cannot
Go back to him; may Afrasyab give me
Safe conduct to wherever God provides.
I'll search throughout the world for some land where
My name will never come to king Kavus,
Where I'll hear nothing of his evil nature,
Where I can rest a while from all his malice.'

So Zangeh and a hundred horsemen took
The hostages from Seyavash's camp;
The look-out at the Turkish capital
220   Caught sight of them—a shout went up and one
Tovorg, a nobleman and warrior,
Went out to welcome them. When Zangeh came

Into the presence of the king, Afrasyab
Rose from his royal throne, embraced him warmly,
Made much of him, assigning him a seat
Of honour. Zangeh sat beside the king,
Gave up his message and went over all
That had been said. When Afrasyab took in
His words he frowned and inwardly he writhed,
His heart was filled with pain. He ordered rooms   230
To be prepared for Zangeh and that he be
Provided for according to his rank.
Piran, his vizir, came; the monarch cleared
The court and told this famous nobleman
About Kavus and all his callow chatter,
His evil and opinionated nature,
His contentiousness—and as he spoke his face
Grew clouded and his heart was filled with grief
For Seyavash. He went in detail through
The embassy of Zangeh, Shavran's son,   240
Then asked, 'What medicine can we bring to this?
What can we do to extricate ourselves
From this dilemma?' And Piran replied,
'May you live for ever, my lord; you're wiser
Than we are in each matter and more able
To do what must be done. In my opinion,
As far as heart and knowledge guide me
There's no well-meaning person in the world,
No one who has the power in private or
In public to assist this prince, who would   250
Deny him either treasure or his trouble.
I've heard that in the world no nobleman's
A match for him in stature, comeliness
And dignity, in wisdom, counsel, honour—
No mother's ever borne before a lord
Of such abilities and understanding.
And now he's proved to be superior
Even to these reports, magnanimous,
A true, chivalric prince; if this were not
The case, he'd not have quarreled with his father   260

And given up the throne and crown, asked you
To grant safe conduct in this way—and all
To save a hundred of our noblemen.
From wisdom's point of view it would look wrong
To let him simply slip through our domains—
Our noblemen would blame you, Seyavash
Himself would be aggrieved. And then Kavus
Is getting old, his days upon the throne
Are numbered; Seyavash is young and glorious,
270 The throne and its prerogatives will all
Be his. So if the king considers this
With forethought, he will write to this wise youth
A letter such as loving fathers send
Their sons—prepare a place for him to live
Within our borders and provide for him
According to his station; give him a girl
In marriage, treat him with consideration
And see he saves his face. And if he stays
Here as our sovereign's guest, your lands and borders
280 Will be at peace; if he goes back again,
You'll still be better off—he'll be made much
Of by Kavus, congratulated by
Their lords. If God should give this prince to us,
Both countries can have done with war—it would
Be worthy of God's justice if He brought
A righteous peace to our war-ravaged world.'
When Afrasyab heard Piran's words, he too
Considered what would happen, weighing in
His mind the good and bad that might result.
290 He answered his old counselor as follows:
'Now everything you've said is welcome to me
But there's an adage that describes this case,
"If you bring up a lion's male cub you'll be
Rewarded when it cuts its teeth—when it's
Developed strength and claws it will attack
The hand that fed it." ' But Piran replied,
'Now may the king of heroes look at this
With wisdom for a moment. Is the man

Who's not inherited his father's malice,
His evil nature, likely to display such 300
Wickedness? Can't you see Kavus is old?
That being old he must die soon? And then
Prince Seyavash will take the spacious world
Into his hands—the palaces and courts,
The treasures, with no trouble, will be his.
Two countries, with their crowns and thrones, will then
Be yours! Well, would you call the man who gained
Them fortunate or not?' When Afrasyab
Heard these remarks he took a wise decision.

AFRASYAB'S LETTER TO SEYAVASH

He called in an experienced scribe who dipped
His pen in ink of ambergris and took
Down everything king Afrasyab dictated.
The king began with praise of God, the world's
Creator, acknowledging His power and wisdom:
'Since He's beyond both time and place, how can
The thoughts of us, His slaves, encompass Him?
He is the Lord of Spirit and of Wisdom,
His justice nourishes the wise—and may
His benediction be upon the prince, 10
Himself the lord of mace and sword and helmet,
Of modesty, religious reverence,
Whose heart and hand are free from crookedness
And all injustice. I have heard your message,
From end to end, from prudent Zangeh, the son
Of Shavran, and my heart is saddened by
This secret animus the world's king has
Against you. But what is there that the wise
And fortunate seek out but crowns and thrones
In all the world? All these, both sovereignty 20
And wealth, await you here and all Turan
Will do you reverence—I myself long for
Your love; now be my son and I'll be like

A father to you, but one who stands before
His son, his sword-belt buckled on for service. [49]
Now understand, Kavus has never—not
For one day—shown you love like mine, I'll open
My locked treasury doors for you, give you a crown
And throne; I'll treat you without harshness, as
30   A father treats his son, and when I die
My memory in the world will live in you.
If you were simply to slip through my country,
Then everyone, both high and low alike,
Would blame me; and, besides, you'd find the going
Beyond my borders difficult, unless
God favored you—there's no land there, you'd have
To cross the Sea of China! But now God
Has made all this unnecessary for you—
Stay here and live in luxury; here troops
40   And treasure and a country wait for you,
You needn't look for an excuse to leave.
And if you think of reconciliation
With your father, I'll give a golden belt
And crown to you, then send you to Iran
Escorted by my troops, and I myself
In friendly sympathy will travel with you.
This quarrel with your father won't last long,
He's old, he'll soon grow tired of disagreements;
When men of sixty-five flare up in fury
50   Their breath's too feeble to sustain the fire—
And then Iran and all its troops and treasures
Are yours, your reign will stretch from land to land.
Besides, I've made a promise before God
That I'll devote my soul and body to
Your welfare; I'll not order, I myself
Will not commit or even in my heart
Consider, any evil act against you.'
When he had sealed the letter, Afrasyab
Commanded Zangeh to be ready for
60   The road and gave him as a gift a cloak
Embroidered all in gold and silver thread,

Together with a horse and splendid trappings.
Zangeh rode like the wind and when he came
To Seyavash's throne he told the prince
What he had asked and heard and seen. Now half
Of Seyavash's heart rejoiced at what
Was said, but half was full of pain and sorrow
That he must make an enemy his friend,
Since how can cooling breezes come from fire?

He wrote a letter to his father then,   70
Recounting everything that had occurred:
'I learnt what wisdom is when young, and I
Have never rushed at either good or evil;
Because that woman—who's so inward with
The king she's like the marrow in his bones—
Made my heart glow with secret shame, the rooms
His women live in were the cause of my
First grief; she forced my heart's blood to my cheeks,
She forced me to traverse a hill of fire,
And in the plains the deer wept tears for me.   80
To get away from this insulting shame
I marched against the monstrous claws of war;
Two countries now are reconciled, at peace;
The king's heart, though, is like a hardened sword
And nothing I do pleases him—I shut,
And he shouts "open"; open, he shouts "shut"![50]
And since the king is sick of seeing me
It's pointless now to linger in his sight.
May his heart never be bereft of joy,
But this calamity has driven me   90
Into a dragon's maw; I do not know
What grief or joy the heavens hide for me.'
And then he said to Bahram, 'Now prepare
To flourish in the world again—I've given
The crown, our tents, our gathered wealth, the throne,
The banners, cavalry, the elephants
We bind our war-drums on into your care
Till Tus, the army's general, comes—and, as

You take them from my hands, see he receives
100   Them all; be vigilant, I wish you well.'
He chose three hundred horsemen from the army
As escort, all battle-worthy warriors,
A hundred horses with their gold-worked trappings,
A hundred slaves with gold-worked belts; he had
The weapons, bridles, belts all counted out,
Along with cash and jewels for his expenses.
He summoned next the army's noblemen
And spoke a few words, as was fitting, to them:
'Piran, most trusted of his tribe, has crossed
110   The Oxus bringing me, from Afrasyab,
A secret message—I must welcome him;
You must stay here and look to Bahram for
Your orders, don't twist your hearts aside
From what he says.' The warriors all kissed
The ground in sign of true submission to
Their noble lord and when the shining sun
Sank in the sky, darkening the air and earth,
Prince Seyavash led his contingent to
The Oxus's shore and from his eyes the tears
120   Flowed down like blood. He reached Termez and there
The decorations put to welcome him
On roofs and in the streets made all the town
Like springtime with their scents and tints—and thus
Each town as far as Chaj seemed like a bride
Decked out with bridal crowns and necklaces;
At every stage fine foods were waiting, carpets
Spread out. And so it was to Qajqarbashi,
Where he dismounted for a while and rested.
As news of his arrival spread a group
130   Of warriors set off with drums to greet him,
Piran picked out a thousand of his men
To organize a suitable reception—
The troops were told the happy news and four
White elephants were sumptuously arrayed;
One bore a howdah glittering with bright turquoise
Surmounted by a banner sapling-high,

Topped by a golden moon—the flag's ground was
Of purple silk, its emblem worked in gold;
The three remaining elephants bore gold
Embroidered howdahs, a hundred lovely girls— 140
With gold-worked belts accompanied them, there were
Besides a hundred noble horses all
With gold-worked saddles draped in fine brocade—
And seeing all this splendid multitude
You'd say the earth was decked with heaven's love.
Hearing of their approach, prince Seyavash
Prepared to meet them—then he saw Piran,
Their leader's banner, heard the trumpeting
Of elephants, the neighing of their horses;
He hurried forward to embrace Piran 150
And questioned him about his glorious king.
He asked him, 'Champion of your troops, why take
Such trouble coming out to welcome me?
The greatest wish my heart has harbored was
To see you with my own eyes safe and sound.'
Piran then kissed his forehead and his feet,
His heart-bewitching face, and said, 'Young prince,
Your coming's like a dream to me, I praise
God now to see you well and in the flesh;
King Afrasyab will be a father to you 160
And everyone on our side of the Oxus
Will be your slave—more than a thousand of
My loyal followers are here like servants
Who wear the earring as a badge of office;
All men and women here will be your slaves,
You will not draw one breath in discontent,
And, if you can accept an old man's service,
I too shall buckle on my belt for you.'
Together they went forward, happily
Discussing this and that, the roads all filled 170
With sounds of harps and lutes—enough to rouse
The deepest sleepers—and the earth made black
With scattered musk and gold, their Arab horses
Sprightly and quick as if they'd sprouted wings.

When Seyavash saw all of this tears flowed
Freely from his eyes and vehemently he thought
Of all the country of Zabolestan—
The beauty of the land that stretches to Kabul;
Then he remembered all Iran and from
180   His inmost entrails heaved an icy sigh.
His heart reviewed Iran and burnt with pain,
His cheeks blushed fiery red—he turned and hid
His face from their commander, wise Piran,
Who saw and understood his pain and sorrow,
Who knew what Seyavash was thinking of
And, deeply moved, bit hard against his lip.
At Qajqarbashi[51] the two of them dismounted
To rest awhile; Piran then gazed at Seyavash,
He wondered at his chest and shoulders, his
190   Demeanor and his speech; he could not tear
His staring eyes from him, repeatedly
He murmured thanks to God. He said, 'Great prince,
You are the living representative
Of all the world's great kings; three attributes
Are yours, no other noble shares all three—
First that you're of the seed of king Qobad
And seem the paragon of all that race,
And second that your tongue speaks only truth
And righteousness, and thirdly that it seems
200   Your face renews the earth itself with love.'
Prince Seyavash replied to him, 'O pure
And reverend, righteous counselor, renowned
Throughout the world for loyalty and love,
The enemy of Ahriman and evil,
If now you'll pledge your word to me, I know
It is a pledge you'll never break; if my
Residing here is right, I should not weep
For what I've done; and if it's wrong, tell me
To leave, point out the road to other lands.'
210   Piran replied, 'Don't think of this—since you
Have left Iran, don't turn your heart away
From Afrasyab's kind hospitality,

Don't be in any hurry to depart.
True, Afrasyab is known throughout the world
As evil, but he's not like this—he is
A godly man: he's wise, intelligent,
Astute, and in no hurry to do harm.
I am related to him[52] and I serve
Both as his champion and his counselor.
More than a hundred thousand horsemen in   220
This land are under my command; I own
Wide territories, herds of horses, flocks
Of sheep, bows, lassoes, all implements of war,
Much more besides that's hidden—I depend
On no one—all this wealth is at your service
If you'll agree to live in happiness
With us; I take you as a trust from God
According to the wishes of the wise,
And swear that nothing evil will befall you;
No man can know the secrets of the heavens,   230
But if you're threatened in our territories,
The antidote for poison will be there.'[53]
Piran's words reassured the prince—he reached
For wine; the two of them sat down to eat,
Piran a father, Seyavash his son.
Then they continued with their journey, laughing,
Light-hearted, wasting no more time, as far
As Gang, the pleasant seat of Afrasyab.

The Turkish king, his sword-belt buckled on,
Came hurrying from the palace to the street;   240
When Seyavash saw Afrasyab on foot,
He too dismounted, running toward the king—
The two embraced; repeatedly each kissed
The other's forehead, eyes, till Afrasyab
Declared, 'The turning of the world is now
At rest, from now on neither civil strife
Nor war will flare up—at the water-hole
The leopard and the lamb will drink together.
The world was plunged in violence by brave Tur,

250 But now the earth's face has grown sick of war,
Our countries have been filled with bitterness,
The world's heart blind to possibilities
Of peace—but now through you the times grow quiet,
Resting from battle and hot-blooded rage;
Now all Turan is as your slave, all hearts
Are filled with love for you; myself and all
I own are yours, Turan's great general[54] stands
Before you now, his soul and body yours.'
Then Seyavash bowed low before the king
260 And said, 'May Fortune ever guard your race,
Thanks be to God from Whom come peace and war
And hatred.' Hand in hand with Seyavash,
King Afrasyab approached the royal throne
And sat, gazing at Seyavash's face,
And said, 'There's no one like him in the world—
No earthly man has such a face, such stature,
Such royal glory.' To Piran he said, 'Kavus
Is rash and foolish to give up a son
Like this, who has such stature and such strength,
270 Such princely ways; now that I've seen him face
To face I wonder at the foolishness
Of one who having such a child could turn
His eyes from him to anything on earth.'
He chose a palace for him, had it spread
With cloth of gold for carpets, end to end;
Its throne was made of gold, the feet shaped like
The heads of oxen; Chinese tapestries
Adorned the walls and countless serving girls
Were summoned; then he ordered Seyavash
280 To go there and to live in joy and glory.
When Seyavash arrived before the building,
He saw its dome reached high as Saturn's sphere—
He entered then and took his place upon
The golden throne, his wise soul wrapped in thought.
The king's meal was prepared and someone came
To summon Seyavash; the talk throughout
The feast ranged everywhere, for everyone

The time passed cheerfully. The banquet over
A place was set aside to sit and drink—
They went escorted by the sound of lutes—
And all the nobles settled to their wine.
Then Afrasyab pledged heart and soul to him—
He'd know no peace if Seyavash were absent.
They drank till all the world grew dark and wine
Had made them tipsy. Then prince Seyavash
Strode to the palace he'd been given—and in
His cheerful drunkenness forgot Iran.
King Afrasyab commanded Shideh, 'Go
To Seyavash when he wakes up—go with
Our champions, people from our family,
The best we have, at early dawn—take slaves
And presents, noble horses, golden bridles,
Have troops bear trays of coins and royal gems
And see they go before him carefully,
With dignity, in silence.' Afrasyab
Sent many gifts; in this way one week passed.

One night the king remarked to Seyavash,
'Let's go tomorrow at first light and play
A polo[55] chukker on the great parade ground,
We can amuse ourselves a while with games—
I've heard from everyone no warrior wants
To face your mallet when you've played at home;
You are my son, the chosen of my court,
The crown of all the Kayanids, the backbone
Of your army.' And Seyavash replied,
'May the king live for ever, your soul gifted
With foresight! Monarchs look to you for guidance—
And who in any matter could surpass you?
The daylight dawns for me when I see you,
From you alone I look for good and evil.'

290

300

310

320

SEYAVASH SHOWS HIS SKILLS BEFORE AFRASYAB

At dawn the Turks approached the playing-field,
Laughing, galloping, curveting their horses;
The Turkish king announced to Seyavash,
We'll choose teams for a chukker, you on that side,
I on this—now let's divide the players up.'
But Seyavash replied, 'How could I use
My mallet in this way? Choose someone else
As your opponent, I can't play against you;
Since, while I'm worthy of the honour, I'm
Your friend I'll ride with you on this broad field.'
The king was pleased by what he said, he thought
All other men's remarks the merest wind;
'Now by the head and soul of king Kavus.'
He said, 'be my opponent in this game—
Display your skills before our horsemen, so that
They don't say, "But he's made a wretched choice"—
And when my men congratulate you, then
My face will blossom with the broadest smiles.'
And Seyavash replied, 'To order's yours;
The men, the field, the mallets—all are yours.'
The king chose Garsivaz, Golbad, Jahan
(Pulad's son), warlike Nastihan, Piran,
Human, whose skill was driving balls from water;
To Seyavash's side he sent men like
Ruin, the famous Shideh, Andariman,
A lion-like horseman he expressly sent for,
Who wrestled his opponents to the ground.
Then Seyavash said, 'My ambitious lord,
Which of these men will dare play well against you?
They're all the king's companions—I will be
Alone, sole player on my side; now if
The king will grant it, I'll have on the field
With me some Persian horsemen from my escort,
And they can be my team for this event
According to the code that rules both sides.'
The king agreed to this and Seyavash
Selected seven skilled Iranian players.

The sound of drums rose from the playing-field,
Dust filled the air and, in the clash of cymbals,
The blare of trumpets, the ground itself seemed shaken.   40
Then Seyavash urged on his horse and, as
He came on to the field, he saw the ball before
Him in the dust and struck it such a blow
It disappeared from sight. The great king ordered
Another ball be brought to Seyavash,
Who as he took it kissed it—and the blare
Of trumpets, the roll of drums, again rang out.
He mounted a fresh horse, threw down the ball
The king had sent and struck it with his mallet
So hard it seemed to rise and greet the moon—   50
The ball just disappeared as if the heavens
Had sucked it up. The king laughed and his nobles,
As though they'd all been roused from sleep, cried out,
'We've seen no finer horseman than this prince.'
To one side of the field they set a throne;
The king approached and took his seat and next
To him sat Seyavash, whose presence pleased
The king enormously. Then he addressed
The teams: 'Field, mallets, balls, are at your service.'
The two teams started and the dust rose up,   60
Ascending to the sun. But when the Turks
Attacked in fury, searching for possession,
The Persians snatched the ball from them so that
Their efforts were quite useless—and Seyavash,
Upset by how his men behaved, called out
In Pahlavi, [56] 'Is this field meant for games
Or war? The match is almost over now;
Hold back and let them have the ball for once!'
The Persian horsemen let their reins hang loosely
And did not heat their horses after this—   70
Then, as the Turks bore down like fire and scored,
King Afrasyab heard their victorious shouts
And realized what that Pahlavi had meant.
He turned to Seyavash and said, 'A friend

Remarked to me that when you square your shoulders
To draw a bow-string back there's no one who
Could be your equal.' When he heard these words
The prince uncased his royal bow; the king
Asked if he might have one of his retainers
Try to draw it; he gazed at it in wonder
And murmured many royal compliments,
Then gave it to the swordsman Garsivaz
And said, 'Bend it and string it!' The warrior
Struggled to string the bow, but had not strength
And sulkily returned it to the prince,
Who took it, knelt, and with his hand bent back
The shaft and strung it. Afrasyab then roared
With laughter, saying, 'There's the bow a man needs!
When I was young I had one just like this—
Well, times are changed, there's no one in Turan
Or in Iran who'd dare take such a bow
To battle with him now; but Seyavash—
With his great chest and shoulders—wouldn't want
To fight with any other!' Then they set
A target in the track where horses race
And Seyavash made no objection but
Bestrode his wind-quick charger like a devil,
Gripped with his thighs and bellowed out his war-cry.
In sight of all the watching warriors he loosed
An arrow and it hit the target's centre,
Immediately he loosed a second shaft,
Of poplar wood, four-feathered—it too struck,
Two arrows in a single charge; he wheeled
His horse round to the right and shot again
At will, then slung his bow across his arm
And cantered over to the noble king
Where he dismounted, and the king stood up,
Calling down blessings on him from above.
They walked together to the towering palace,
Their hearts made happy by their mutual love,
Sat down to eat and called for wine, inviting
Those worthy of the honour to sit with them;

The wine went down in quantities, the group
Grew tipsy-drunk and toasted Seyavash.
Whilst they were at the banquet Afrasyab
Arranged for gifts for Seyavash—a robe
Of honour, horses, bridles, thrones and crowns,
And bolts of uncut cloth of gold, the like
Of which no man had seen before, coins, cash
In purses, garnets, turquoise, other gems   120
Of various kinds, a multitude of slave-girls,
As many slave-boys, and a goblet filled
With glowing rubies. He gave orders that
The wealth be counted out and carried to
The palace he'd conferred on Seyavash—
His kinsmen in Turan were to increase
The kindness and respect they felt for him;
He said to them, 'You are to think of him
As if you were the flock and he your shepherd.'
And to the prince himself he said, 'One day   130
You must come hunting with me—it'll set
Our hearts at rest and we'll enjoy ourselves,
Our hunt will cure all sorrows of the soul.'
He answered him, 'Wherever you decide,
And in whatever way your heart desires.'

And so one day they set out for the hunt;
The king took hawks and cheetahs, and a group
Of men of all ranks from Turan and from
Iran accompanied him. Prince Seyavash
Saw on the plain a herd of onager—   140
Quick as the wind he left the group behind,
His bridle slack, he stood tall in the stirrups,
Then with a sword blow split an onager
In two, and with his hands he weighed the halves
(His hands a balance and the meat like silver)
And neither half was one grain heavier than
The other. When the king's men saw this they
As one man cried, 'Now here's the prince of swordsmen!'
To one another though they said, 'Our lord

150   Is put to shame, this is an evil chance
      That's reached us from Iran; it would be right
      If we opposed the king in this affair.'
      The prince urged on his horse, pursuing game
      Across the wastes, through mountains, caves and plains,
      With sword and lance and arrow; and everywhere
      He went he left a pile of carcasses,
      Sufficient food for all the group who'd come.
      Light-heartedly they left the hunting-grounds
      And made their way back to the royal palace.
160   Now, whether sad or cheerful, Afrasyab
      Was always closeted with Seyavash,
      Consulting neither Garsivaz, Jahan,
      Or any other of his entourage—
      But it was always Seyavash, both day
      And night, on whom he smiled. And so a year
      With all its mingled joy and grief went by.

                HOW PIRAN AND SEYAVASH BECAME RELATED

      One day Piran and Seyavash were sat
      Together and their talk ranged back and forth;
      Piran remarked to him, 'You're like a man
      Who's merely traveling through our territories—
      Despite the fact that Afrasyab feels such
      Affection for you that he says your name
      When he's asleep; and you should realize that
      You're like the spring to him, that you're his idol.
      The solace of his sorrows. And, besides,
10   You are a nobleman, Kavus's son,
      Your talents lift your head up to the moon.
      Your father's old, your heart's still young, but see
      You don't let this imperial crown evade
      Your grasp. You are the prince of both Iran
      And of Turan, one whose nobility
      Recalls the great kings of the past—now give
      Your heart to this land, build a city here,

A place where you can live in peace and pleasure;
I see no relatives around you, kin
To cherish you, no brothers, sisters, wives—   20
You're like a single flower by the wayside.
Look for a wife, a girl who's worthy of you,
Forget your pain and sorrow for Iran;
Once king Kavus has died Iran is yours,
Its royal crown and warrior's throne are yours.
Our king has three girls, lovely as the moon,
Bedecked with jewels, in purdah here—
And if you've seen the moon eclipsed it is
Because it could not tear its eyes from them;
And in his harem Garsivaz has three   30
Girls too, of noble lineage on both sides,
Descendants of great Faridun, all crowned
Princesses of high rank and royal wealth—
Though it would be more suitable for you
To try for one of Afrasyab's own daughters.
And I've four girls myself in purdah here
Each ready to declare herself your slave;
The eldest is called Jarireh, a child
Of unmatched beauty—when she's arrayed in all
Her finery she's like the glittering moon.   40
She won't consider anyone that she
Herself has not decided on, and no
Face pleases her, my noble prince, but yours;
If you agree, she'll be a slave to you,
A girl who stands before you at your service.'
And Seyavash replied, 'I'm grateful to you,
Consider me as closer than a son—
If she will be my soul's and body's solace,
It's her alone I want of those you mention;
You lay on me a debt of gratitude so   50
That I shall not forget until I die.'
Piran then took his leave of Seyavash
And hurried home to find his wife, Golshahr,
And said to her, 'Prepare our Jarireh
To be the bride of glorious Seyavash!

Our son-in-law's to be the grandson of.
Qobad, how can we not rejoice today?'
Golshahr brought in her daughter, set a crown
Upon her head and dressed her in brocade
Bespangled with gold coins and pearls—all that
Was necessary she did, arraying her
With lovely tints and scents so that she seemed
An image of the happiness of spring;
That night she sent her to the prince's arms.
They married her to Seyavash, and when
She sat in state she glittered like the moon;
No one could count her dowry's wealth, the rubies,
The gem-encrusted crowns. When Seyavash
Looked on her face she pleased him and he smiled
And gave himself to pleasure; day and night
He spent delighting in her company,
Unmindful of Kavus and his deceit.

In this way, for a while, the heavens smiled
On Seyavash, and all the time his standing,
Repute and honour with the king increased.
One day Piran, to make things even better,
Remarked to him, 'My lord, you know you are
The light that guides our king's soul day and night—
He leads the armies of Turan, his crown
Surpasses highest heaven's height, and you
To him are as his heart, his consciousness,
His strength, his power. If you could make yourself
A member of his family, your might
Would then grow greater with each breath you drew,
His confidence in you would be increased,
Since you would be more firmly his—and, since
My daughter is your wife, your welfare's of
The first concern to me. Now Farigis
Is loveliest of all the king's young daughters—
In all the world you won't see such a face,
Such hair—her slender stature's finer than
The straightest cypress's, her head is crowned

With musky jet-black curls, her knowledge, her
Accomplishments, are more than can be reckoned,
And Wisdom stands before her as her slave.
It would be fitting if you asked her hand
In marriage from king Afrasyab—in all
Kashmir, in all Kabul, you won't find such
A beauty. Then the noble king would be
Your kinsman and your glory would shine brighter;   100
Just give the order and I'll talk to him,
And so win credit from him for myself.'
Prince Seyavash looked at Piran and said,
'What God wills cannot be denied; if this
Is heaven's purpose, I've no strength to stand
Against its force—and if I'm not to reach
Iran again, or see Kavus's face,
Or that of Zal who brought me up, or that
Of Rostam which was like the brightness of
The spring to me, or Bahram's face, or Zangeh's,   110
Or those of any of our famous heroes—
Since I must needs be severed from their sight
And choose a place to live within Turan—
Act as my father and arrange this match,
But go about it secretly. If Fortune
Wishes me well, she'll clear the way to this
Relationship with Afrasyab.' He spoke,
The lashes of his eyes grew wet with tears
And an icy sigh escaped him. Then Piran
Replied, 'The wise man doesn't fight with Fate;   120
You can't elude the circling of the heavens
From which come peace and war and love; if you
Had friends once in Iran, you left them there,
You gave them up in coming to Turan;
Your life and livelihood are here, although
Iran's great throne remains within your grasp.'

This said, he rose and left the prince, and now
He was aware of Seyavash's wishes
He hurried in high spirits to the palace

130　Where he dismounted and a way was cleared;
　　　He stood a while respectfully before
　　　The throne until his well-intentioned king
　　　Enquired, 'What do you mean by standing here
　　　Before me for so long? What in the world
　　　Do you require? My army and the door
　　　That guards my treasury are at your service
　　　Since what you do has always turned out well.
　　　If there's some prisoner whom I keep in chains,
　　　Even some wretch whose manumission might
140　Prove dangerous to me, well I release
　　　The man, both from my chains and from my anger—
　　　For your sake all my fury's turned to air.
　　　Now what should it be? A trifle or some
　　　Great affair? Ask and it's yours, whether sword,
　　　Seal, crown, or throne.' The wise Piran replied,
　　　'So may the world enjoy your rule for ever!
　　　I have sufficient wealth and troops and treasure,
　　　And in the shadow of your Fortune wield
　　　The power of sword and crown and throne; I bring
150　From Seyavash a lengthy message for
　　　The royal ear. He said to me, "Go to
　　　The Turkish king and say, 'Joy fills my heart,
　　　Ambition fires me; like a father you
　　　Have nourished me within your arms, the fruit
　　　Of your good Fortune is my happiness;
　　　I ask one further favor from you now,
　　　Since I depend on you for everything—
　　　Arrange a match for me. In purdah you've
　　　A daughter worthy of my throne and palace;
160　Her mother calls her Farigis, and I
　　　Shall find my happiness deserving her.' " '
　　　Then Afrasyab grew grave, tears filled his eyes;
　　　He said, 'I've been through this with you before,
　　　Then too you didn't see things as I see them;
　　　A wise man said to me once—and he was
　　　A learned person, of extensive knowledge—
　　　"Why try to educate a lion's whelp?

You're laying on yourself a hopeless task."
Besides, before the council of our nobles,
And in my presence as this young girl's father,   170
Astrologers went through the matter point
By point and said that from the union of
Our tribes a prince would come who'd seize the world
Within his grasp, that nothing would remain
Of all Turan's domains, and that my crown
Would be the first objective of his vengeance;
And I believe the truth was spoken here
Of what the turning heavens hold in store.
Why should I, with my own hands, plant a tree
Whose roots are bitter as the colocynth,   180
Whose fruit will be a poison? A child born from
The seed of Afrasyab and king Kavus
Will be like fire, or like an ocean wave
In its destructive force, and I don't know
If he will smile on our Turan or turn
His face toward Iran. But why should I
Quite consciously drink poison down? One must
Not carelessly pick snakes up by the tail!'
Piran replied to him, 'Your Majesty,
Don't plague yourself with such ideas; the child   190
That's born to Seyavash will be reserved,
Intelligent and wise. Don't trust the talk
Of these astrologers—act prudently,
And see that Seyavash is satisfied.
From these two families a hero will
Be born whose head will be exalted to
The shining sun, he'll be the lord of both
Iran and our Turan, both countries will
Find peace through him. And if unknown to us
The heavens will otherwise, your cautious plans   200
Won't make them kinder, since what the heavens desire
Must be, and all your scruples cannot lessen
The fate that's now maturing there. But look,
This is a glorious opportunity,
The answer to the prayers men pray to Fortune!

And there can be no greater lineage than
The seed of Faridun and Kay Qobad.'
The king replied to him, 'Since your advice
Is never evil in its outcome, I am
210 Convinced by what you say; go now and do
What must be done, and do it well.' Piran
Made his obeisance, bowing low before
The king, and then departed, hurrying
To Seyavash, where he recounted for
Him everything that had occurred. That night
The two sat down together cheerfully
And washed all sorrow from their souls with wine.

HOW AFRASYAB AND SEYAVASH BECAME RELATED

When like a golden shield the sun had raised
Its head into the sky, Piran put on
His sword-belt, mounted a swiftly trotting horse,
And set his face towards Seyavash's palace;[57]
He called down blessings on the prince's glory
And said, 'Prepare yourself today to welcome
King Afrasyab's young daughter here; and if
You give the order, I'll do everything
To see that she's escorted properly.'
10 Prince Seyavash's heart was deeply troubled,
He blushed to see Piran and said, 'Go then,
And do whatever must be done—you know
That I've no secrets from you.' When Piran
Heard this he hurried to his house and threw
Himself into the business heart and soul.
He gave Golshahr[58]—his shrewd and widely praised
Chief wife—the key to where he kept their bolts
Of uncut cloth. They chose the best things in
The treasury—a thousand bolts of cloth,
20 Gold-worked, of Chinese manufacture; emerald-
Encrusted dishes, goblets studded with turquoise
And filled with musk, and aloes wood; two crowns

Covered in princely jewels, two bracelets, a torque,
Two royal earrings; sixty camel-loads
Of carpets, three sets of clothes of cloth of gold,
Embroidered with designs in redder gold
And sewn with jewels; plus thirty camel-loads
Of gold and silver, trays and Persian cloth,
A golden throne, four lesser thrones, three sets
Of golden slippers, their designs picked out   30
In emeralds; then three hundred servants with
Gold coronets, a hundred from their own house,
Twice sixty slaves all bearing golden cups,
A hundred trays of musk, a hundred more
Of saffron, all entrusted to the servants—
This army of retainers brought the dowry
And in their midst a golden palanquin
With curtains of brocade. Golshahr had with her
Some thirty thousand dinars to scatter to
The waiting crowd—and as they brought the wealth   40
To Farigis they called down blessings on her.
Piran and Afrasyab, for their part, bustled
With preparations for prince Seyavash—
Now everyone came forward, for a week
Not even fish or fowl could sleep with all
The turmoil and the world from end to end
Became a paradisal garden filled
With gladness and the sounds of singers' voices.
The marriage contract was drawn up and witnessed,
And when it had been ratified Piran   50
Dispatched a messenger, as quick as smoke,
To Golshahr, saying, 'Now send Farigis,
This very night, to Seyavash's palace;'
Piran's wife, when she heard the message, went
To Farigis; she kissed the ground and said,
'The sun now marries Venus—now, tonight,
You must be with the prince and like the moon
Give splendor to his court.' And like the new
Moon Farigis approached her young crowned prince.

60   A week of celebrations passed; the king
        Arranged for many presents to be sent—
        Sheep, Arab horses, armor, helmets, swords,
        Lassoes, gold coins and purses filled with coins,
        Fine clothes and other gifts, both great and small.
        And then a royal charter was inscribed
        On silk, conferring sovereignty of all
        The towns and lands that stretched from there as far
        As China's sea on Seyavash, and the king
        Sent to the prince's palace a golden throne
70   And crown. A public banquet was decreed
        And everyone who came from near and far
        Found wine and cooks at work—they ate and took
        Back home whatever they could carry with them;
        For one whole happy week they lived as guests
        Of Afrasyab. The prison doors were opened
        In honour of the prince's royal Fortune
        And he rejoiced to see it. At daybreak on
        The eighth day Seyavash, together with
        The noble knight Piran, came to the king.
80   The two made their obeisance and then said,
        'O lord and king of all this land, may all
        Your days be spent in happiness and may
        The backs of all your enemies be bent
        With shame!' They left the palace in high spirits
        And all their talk was praise of Afrasyab.

        Thus for a year the circling heavens turned,
        Conferring love and justice on the world.
        A friendly messenger came from the king
        To Seyavash and said, 'The king greets you
90   As sovereign, saying, "Noble lord, it would
        Be right for you to separate yourself
        From me somewhat, to settle somewhere else;
        I've given you the land from here to China—
        Go on a tour of all your territories
        And, when you find a town that pleases you,
        Where things are to your liking and you feel

At ease, make that your home and give yourself
Unstintingly to happiness and splendor." '
Prince Seyavash was pleased by what he said—
He had the bugles blown, the drums strike up,   100
The baggage-train prepared; an escort brought
Their arms, together with his seal and crown,
Along the way. Unnumbered litters were
Made ready for the women; Farigis
Was placed in one of them, the loads were set,
And Seyavash led out the caravan.
Piran, a man who had no enemies,
And many famous lords, accompanied them;
They travelled cheerfully towards Khotan,
Piran's land, where the prince stayed for a month,   110
An honored guest, as had been promised him.
The young man's days were spent in feasting, or
At ease with wine and music, or out hunting.
Then at the month's end, as the cock's crow sounded,
Drums also sounded and the prince set out
Towards his territories, preceded by
Piran and followed by his troops. As news
Spread through the land its chieftains came to greet
Their overlord; they travelled from their homes
With happy hearts and decked the world with splendor—   120
Such clamor went up from his realm you'd say
The earth had been transported to the heavens;
Such celebrations, such a blaring of
The trumpets that it seemed men's hearts would leap
Out from their chests. They reached a settled place,
A beautiful, well-favored site—to one
Side was the sea, behind the mountains rose,
Not far away were well-stocked hunting-grounds;
Thickly wooded, supplied with flowing streams,
The place made old men's hearts feel young again.   30
Prince Seyavash exclaimed then to Piran,
'This is a lovely site indeed! I'll build
A noble city here, a place to teach
Me how I can rejoice; the town I raise

Will be magnificent, a place that's filled
With palaces and gardens; my capital
Will be exalted to the moon, to make
It worthy of my royal crown and throne.'
Piran replied, 'You're wise and you should follow
140   Wherever your ideas might lead; if you
Command me, I'll raise up a town to reach
The moon, exactly as you wish; I now
Want neither land nor wealth; because of you
Both time and place are worthless to me now.'
Prince Seyavash replied, 'O Fortune's friend,
It's you who make the tree of greatness flourish;
My wealth and welfare come from you alone
And everywhere I see you struggling first
On my behalf. I'll build a town here such
150   That all who see it will stand lost in wonder.'
They turned back from this lovely spot; the prince
Was troubled and he asked astrologers,
'If I should raise a town here, will it bring
Me luck and glory, or breed war and strife
Together they replied, 'This site is not
Sufficiently auspicious for a town.'
The prince was angered by the astrologers,
His heart was filled with pain, his eyes with tears,
Remembering he'd been told before that as
160   The heavens turned they'd bring him finally
A bitter fate. The reins slipped from his hands
And in his eyes warm tears welled up. Piran
Said, 'Prince, what is it that distresses your
And he replied, 'High heaven has filled my heart
With pain and made my soul contemptible—
Whatever wealth I gather, treasure or
Jeweled crowns, will be at last my enemy's;
Evil will triumph and death will come to me. [59]
I'm not long for this world now; in my place
170   Another man will reign and neither I
Nor any son of mine nor any young
Heroic warrior of my race will live

In happiness. My life will not last long,
I'll not need palaces and courtyards soon;
My throne will then be Afrasyab's and death
Will come to take me though I'm innocent;
Such is the will of heaven, raising man
One moment up to glory and the next
Destroying him.' Piran replied, 'My lord,
Why brood so fruitlessly and for so long?   180
You wear the royal signet on your finger
And Afrasyab's your bulwark against evil;
And while my soul's still in my body I
Will do my best to keep my oath to you—
I will not let the winds of heaven blow'
Against you, or the breeze number your hairs.'
Prince Seyavash replied, 'My friend, renowned
For righteousness, whose only goal I see,
Is righteousness, you've sworn an oath, your mind
Is honest, but the heavens will otherwise;   190
My secrets are all known to you and may
They keep your heart alert, your body safe.
I bring you tidings from the court of God,
I know the secrets of the turning skies;
I tell you, truly, what must be, so that,
When I must leave my halls and palaces
And you perceive the way the world turns out,
You won't cry, "Why was all of this concealed
From Seyavash?" Wisest of warriors, Piran,
Open your ears to what I have to say;   200
Not many days will pass before I shall
Though innocent, be murdered wretchedly
By our shrewd-hearted king; another will
Adorn this crown and throne; through my bad Fortune
And through the calumny of one who hates me
My guiltless head will meet an evil fate.
This murder will make life intolerable,
Iran and your Turan will rise against
Each other and from end to end the earth
Will fill with pain; then vengeful swords will swarm   210

Through both our countries; in Iran and in
Turan you'll see so many banners raised—
Red, yellow, purple, black—such pillaging
And plundering, such scattering of wealth
Long hoarded; then how many provinces
Will horses' trampling hooves destroy, while all
The water in their streams turns salt and brackish!
What lamentations will rise up then from
Iran and from Turan! My spilt blood will
220   Convulse the world. Almighty God Who rules
The earth has written in the heavens thus—
And by His order what is sown is reaped.
The Turks' great leader will repent of what
He's done and said, but penitence will be
Of no avail when smoke is rising from
His sacked towns. Come, since when we have to die
We die, let's give ourselves to joy and feasting.'
Piran, when he had heard the prince's words,
Grew pensive and his heart was filled with pain.
230   He speculated, 'If what he declares
Is true, I've brought an evil on myself,
Since it was me who dragged him to Turan;
I've scattered seeds of hatred through the world;
I thought the king's words so much wind, he too
Repeatedly said things like this to me.'
Then inwardly he said, 'But who knows what
The secret turnings of the heavens are?
Who's told him all these mysteries? His thoughts
Are with Iran, Kavus, the royal throne—
240   He's thinking of his former days of greatness.'
He set his heart at rest with these reflections,
Neglecting to pursue the matter wisely.
And all the journey passed in talk like this,
Their hearts filled with foreboding for the future.
But then, dismounting from their horses, they
Had done with their discussions for a while,
Ordered a golden table to be spread
And called for wine, musicians and their lutes;

They spent a week in feasting, telling tales
Of ancient kings. The eighth day came and with it   250
A message to Piran, commander of
The Turkish armies, from king Afrasyab
Saying, 'Press on as far as China's sea,
From there approach Makran and India's borders,
The Sea of Send, demanding tribute as
You go—and with the army overrun
The marches of Khazar.' A shout went up
From great Piran's pavilion and the ground
Shook with the roll of drums; from every side
Pugnacious troops were gathered in huge numbers.   260
Then when the time for their farewells had come
He left a store of treasure, coins and horses
With rich ornaments in Seyavash's care
While he himself, as he'd been ordered, led
The army out on their grand expedition.

At nightfall at about the time men sleep,
A messenger as quick as spreading fire
Arrived from Afrasyab; he brought a letter
Emblazoned like the turning heavens and filled
With kindest sentiments for Seyavash.   270
It said, 'Since you departed I have known
No joy, my every moment's filled with grief;
But I've sought out a site that's worthy of you
Here in Turan; however happy you
Might be where you are now—and may your heart
Stay free of care, your life be prosperous
And fortunate, your slanderers filled with sorrow—
Return now to my kingdom and reduce
The heads of those who hate you to the dust.'
Then Seyavash assembled all his army   280
And quickly set out as the king had ordered.
He had a hundred camels loaded down
With treasure, forty more with cash in dinars,
A thousand red-haired Bactrian camels made up
The baggage-train; ten thousand hand-picked swordsmen,

Both from Iran and from Turan, rode with him;
The litters for the ladies, together with
The valuables (the rubies, royal gems,
Torques, crowns, earrings, musk, camphor, aloes wood,
290   Perfumes, rich brocades, silk furnishings, goods
Of Chinese, Persian and Egyptian make),
All packed on thirty camels, led the train.
When he'd arrived at the appointed site
Prince Seyavash marked out an area
Two parasangs in length by two in breadth
And built a city like a paradise
With audience halls, tall castles, open squares,
Orchards and lovely gardens filled with flowers;
And in the wilderness he planted roses,
300   Wild hyacinths and tulips. His audience chamber
Had various paintings—scenes that showed great kings,
Their banquets and their battles—on the walls;
Here Rostam, blessed with elephantine strength,
Sat on his throne, surrounded by Gudarz
And Zal and all his court; there Afrasyab
Was shown with his retainers, warriors like
Piran and unforgiving Garsivaz.
At every corner rose a cupola
Whose summit touched the clouds; and there
210   Among the stars musicians sat and sang.
They called the city Seyavashkard[60]—it was
A place that pleased all hearts within the province.

Piran returned from India and China
And all men's talk was praise of this new town
Called Seyavashkard, renowned throughout Turan
For all its audience halls, its palaces,
Its orchards and its gardens, for the plain
Where it was built, the river and the mountains,
And founded on a day the stars decreed
320   As suitable.[61] Impatience seized Piran
To see what Seyavash had done with this
Illustrious site, and when he started out

He brought a thousand of his finest warriors,
The best men of the region, men worthy of
The honour. As Piran came near the site
Prince Seyavash went with his retinue
To welcome him; Piran saw Seyavash
Approaching in the distance and dismounted—
The prince dismounted from his blue-black horse
And held the warrior tightly in his arms;   330
The two then toured the city; tales were told
Of every gateway's workmanship, they viewed
From end to end the gardens, public squares
And palaces, on every side they saw
Resplendent buildings rise; the army's chief
Piran went everywhere and as he went
He heaped unstinted praises on the prince.
He said, 'If royal power and its authority
Together with your wisdom'd not been yours,
How could you have begun to build this place   340
Or founded such a town? May this be your
Memorial among the brave until
The day of resurrection comes, and may
The splendid race of your descendants live
In glory here, from son to son, world-conquering
And victorious.' When Piran had seen a part
Of this propitious town they reached the court
And gardens of prince Seyavash; from there
Piran's triumphal route continued to
The palace of queen Farigis, who came   350
To greet him, scattering coins before his feet.
Enthroned, he looked around and saw the place
Was like a heart-delighting paradise;
He praised it handsomely and rendered thanks
To God, the world's creator. Then they fell
To feasting, wine, fine food, the services
Of cooks and cup-bearers. They spent a week
With wine cups in their hands—at times rejoicing,
At times quite drunk. Next, when the eighth day came,
Piran produced the presents he'd collected   360

While traveling, all worthy gifts like rubies
And royal jewels, cash, gem-encrusted crowns,
Silks, horses with gold trappings, saddles made
From leopard skins, the pommels carved from poplar.
To Farigis he gave a crown and earrings,
A bracelet and a necklace worked with jewels.
He left then in good spirits with his men
And travelled to Khotan; when he arrived,
Happy to be at home, he went at once
370   Into the harem, where he told Golshahr,
'Whoever has not seen or does not know
The joys Rezvan's[62] reserved for men in heaven
Should take the trouble now to travel—he'd
Be well rewarded—to the city built
By Seyavash; its lord is lovelier than
The place he's made and sits upon his throne
Bright as the sun upon Sorush's[63] throne,
Illuminating all the east with brilliance.'
From there, as swiftly as a skiff on water,
380   He went to Afrasyab and told him all
He'd done and where, the taxes he'd collected—
He brought them all before the king and gave
Him detailed news of all his territories
And said, 'From China's sea to that of Rome
Our king's just rule has made all regions flourish.'
He mentioned next prince Seyavash and told
His monarch everything he'd seen; the king
For his part questioned him about the prince,
His town, his province and his court. Piran
390   Replied, 'Whoever sees the spring's sweet joys
In Paradise could not distinguish them
From Seyavash's city, or its lord
From heaven's sun; it is as if Sorush
Instructed him on how to keep the province—
I saw a city there the like of which
No man has seen in China or Turan,
So many gardens, palaces and streams
You'd say the mind that planned it all

Had supernatural wisdom. [64] From far off
I saw the palace of queen Farigis   400
Which glittered like a treasury of jewels
Laid out at a festival. Your son-in-law
Is as your heart would wish, a man of grace
And dignity; it's right that men complain
And freely too, of this capricious world,
But you have no cause for complaint—if from
The heavens Sorush himself descended, he
Could not have managed matters with more wit,
Magnificence and pomp. Besides, he's made
Two countries rest from war, they're quiet now   410
Like some great lord who's been restored to reason.
May men like him with wisdom in their hearts
And righteous minds be with us here for ever!'
Delighted at the news his son-in-law's
Abilities had borne such fruit, the king
Told Garsivaz of all Piran had said
And then revealing everything he knew
He said to him, with measured seriousness,
'Go now to Seyavashkard, examine all
You find there; Seyavash has given his heart   420
To this land, to Turan, he never thinks
Now of Iran and it's as if he'd said
Farewell both to his royal crown and throne
And to Bahram, Gudarz and king Kavus.
Look, in the thorn-brakes he has made a city,
A fruitful province filled with happiness,
He's built tall palaces for his dear queen,
Beloved Farigis. And when you meet,
Address him with appropriate respect,
Look on his face with magnanimity.   430
When drinking, or out hunting on the plains,
You'll have a group of Persians to attend you,
When you remember me, drink to my name
Then fall to your pleasures. See you prepare
An ample quantity of presents for him—
Coins, horses, gold-worked belts, jewels, thrones,

Chinese brocades, armlets, maces, swords, seal-rings,
Carpets, all that's brightly colored and smells sweet;
Off with you now and see whatever you
440   Can lay your hands on in our treasury,
Find similar presents for queen Farigis,
And greet them both with praise; if Seyavash
Proves he's a good host and he welcomes you,
Stay in his happy city for two weeks.'
The noble Garsivaz picked out ten thousand
Turkish horsemen and with this splendid troop
He set out, in high spirits, for Seyavashkard.

GARSIVAZ VISITS SEYAVASH

When Seyavash had news of his approach
He and a group of soldiers galloped out
To welcome him; the two embraced, the prince
Asked Garsivaz about the king, and then
They went on to the palace where living quarters
Were set aside for Garsivaz's escort.
The next day dawned and Garsivaz appeared
Before the prince, presenting him with gifts,
A robe of honour sent by Afrasyab.
10   When Seyavash saw what he had been given
He blushed and smiled, his face a rose in springtime.
He took his guest around the city and showed
Him all the buildings one by one before
They turned back to the palace. But just then
A horseman rode up, quickly as the wind,
To Seyavash—he brought good news, and said,
'The daughter of our mighty warrior[65]
Has borne a baby who's the image of
Your majesty!—they've called the boy Forud.
20   It happened in the darkness of the night,
But when Piran got news of it, at once
He sent me and another horseman here
Saying, "Be off, and tell the prince our news!

Queen Jarireh, the noblest of our ladies,
The baby's mother, told her maids to smear
The infant's hand with saffron and to press it
Hard on this letter, saying, 'Take this sign
To Seyavash, who's subject to no ruler.
And tell him though I've now grown old, my God
Has granted me this moment's happiness.' "   30
Prince Seyavash replied, 'I pray this child
And his descendants occupy the throne
For ever!' The messenger was then rewarded with
So many coins the slave who brought them bent,
Exhausted by their weight.[66] Light-heartedly
They went on to the court of Farigis,
The nobly born, and saw her—crowned, enthroned,
And served by slaves with golden diadems.
She came down from her throne and welcomed them,
Then questioned Garsivaz about the king,   40
Her father, and her home. But Garsivaz
Seethed in his heart and brain, his outward manner
Dissembling his thoughts. Inwardly he murmured,
'A few more years of this and Seyavash
Will not consider anyone worth knowing;
Crown, throne, sovereignty, treasure, wisdom, troops—
They're all his now.' Within he writhed in rage,
Although his sallow face did not betray
The secrets of his heart. To Seyavash
He said, 'You've profited from all your troubles,   50
May you enjoy this wealth for many years.'
Two thrones were set up in the golden hall
And there both lords, rejoicing in good fortune,
Were entertained; cup-bearers and musicians
Appeared before the gem-encrusted thrones
And Garsivaz allowed his heart to be
Beguiled by singers' voices, harps and lutes.

The shining sun disclosed its secret power
And showed its face to all the world below.
Prince Seyavash went to the playing-field   60

And rode around it, practicing his game;
Then Garsivaz arrived and threw the ball,
Which Seyavash pursued—he struck it smartly,
But his opponent's stick struck only dust
That spurted from the course; the ball the prince
Struck disappeared, as if the sky had sucked
It up. He ordered that a golden throne
Be placed beside the field and that his men
Contest with lances; quickly as a wind
70   The horsemen filled the field, their lances couched
For combat—from the golden throne both nobles
Watching to see who'd gain the greatest glory.
Then Garsivaz said, 'O my lord, your talents
Remind us of the prowess of past kings,
Your skill exceeds the greatness of your birth—
It would be right for you to show the Turks
A sample of your mastery for once
With sharpened spears and arrows.' Seyavash
In token of agreement laid his hand
80   Upon his chest; he changed his throne then for
The saddle and they bound five suits of mail
Firmly all together, each one of them
Weighty enough to tire a man, and placed
Them at the field's end while the army watched
From every side. Prince Seyavash took up
A royal spear that he'd been given by
His father (who had used it hunting lions
And in the war against Mazanderan);
He rode out to the course they'd made, his spear
90   In one hand and the reins tight round the other,
Then like a maddened elephant he charged;
He thrust the spear in, lifting up the armor
— And not a knot or fastening stayed intact—
Then with a flourish flung the suits at will
About the field. Prince Garsivaz's horsemen
Searched through the course with spears, examining
The suits, but did not find a single one
Whose fastenings had survived. Next, Seyavash

Asked that four shields made in Gilan be brought,
Two wooden, two of tempered iron; he called then   100
For his bow and arrows made of poplar wood—
He thrust six in his belt, three more he held
And notched one on the bow-string; with his thighs
He gripped his horse and charged, and in the sight
Of all the army shot the arrow through
All four shields, wood and iron alike; he shot
Ten arrows in this way and young and old
Cried their congratulations; of the ten
That Seyavash let fly there was not one
That did not pierce the shields, and every man   110
Who saw the feat invoked God's blessings on him.
'O prince, you have no equal in Iran
Or in Turan,' said Garsivaz. 'Come now,
Let's you and I—in front of all this army—
As wrestling champions grasp each other's belts. [67]
Just as you'll not see many horses equal
To mine, so there's no Turkish warrior who's
My equal; you on your side have no match
In prowess and in stature—and if I
Can seize you from your saddle unawares   120
And hurl you to the ground, it's proof that I'm
The better warrior, that my horse and might
Beat yours; if you can throw me on the ground,
I'll not ride round a battlefield again.'
But Seyavash replied, 'Don't say such things—
You are a prince, a lion, a fierce contender,
Your horse is like a king compared to mine,
Your helmet's like Azargoshasp[68] to mine!
So choose another Turk, besides yourself,
To fight with me in friendly competition!'   130
And Garsivaz replied, 'Ambitious lord,
What could be shown by such a friendly match?'
But Seyavash said, 'Combat between brothers
Is wrong—in combat though men smile their hearts
Are filled with rage; you are the king's own brother,
Your horse's hooves tread down the moon itself—

I'll do whatever you command, but I'll
Not break our fellowship by such an act!
Choose some brave lion from your companions, set him
On this light-footed horse and, if you're still
Determined I should fight, you'll see the heads
Of your proud warriors humbled in the dust.'
Ambitious Garsivaz was pleased by what
He said and smiled and, turning to his Turks,
Announced, 'Proud warriors! Which of you would wish
To have his name renowned throughout the world?
Who will be matched with Seyavash and lay
The chief of haughty fighters in the dust?'
His listeners' lips were locked, till Gerui,
The son of Zereh, spoke, 'If he has no
Opponent, I'm his match!' When Seyavash
Heard Gerui's remark, he frowned, his soul
Was troubled; Garsivaz said, 'Well, my lord,
No warrior in the army's this man's equal!'
But Seyavash replied, 'Unless I fight
With you, combat for me's contemptible—
Two champions should be chosen for the contest
And on the field I'll fight against them both.'
There was a well-known warrior called Damur,
A man unequalled for his strength among
The Turks, and he came forward, ready for
The contest with the royal Persian prince.
Then Seyavash prepared to fight; Damur
And Gerui wheeled round him—Seyavash
Grabbed at the belt of Gerui, his fist
Closed on the buckle and he hurled him from
The saddle to the ground, he had no need
Of mace or lariat. Next, he turned to face
Damur and caught him in a tight embrace
About the neck and chest, lifting him lightly
Up from the saddle, so that all the army
Was astonished—and thus he bore the man
To Garsivaz as easily as if
No warrior chief were tucked beneath his arm!

140

150

160

170

Then he dismounted, opened up his arms,
And sat down laughing on his golden throne.
But Garsivaz was furious with the prince,
His face flushed and his heart was filled with pain;
They left the throne and went back to the palace,
And some among them cursed the Persian prince.   180

They spent a week with music, flutes and lutes,
Wine, entertainers, luxury—until
The eighth day came and Garsivaz and all
His noble retinue prepared to leave.
The prince composed a letter full of friendship
And kind enquiries to king Afrasyab
To which he added many gifts, so that
The travelers left the city in good spirits.
But as they went they talked to one another
About the noble prince and his domains,   190
And Garsivaz, who looked to stir up trouble,
Said, 'From Iran an evil's come to us;
The king has summoned someone from Iran
Who puts us all to shame—two lion-warriors,
Damur and Gerui, these two fierce fighters,
Were made contemptible, ridiculous,
All by this single filthy horseman's fist;
And this won't be the end of it—I see
No sense in this affair he's brought on us!'
And so the channel flowed with muddied water   200
Until they reached the court of Afrasyab.

When they appeared before Turan's chief warrior
He plied the group with questions; Garsivaz
Answered at length and gave the king the letter,
Who read it, laughed, and was delighted with it.
But Garsivaz, whom rancor filled, noticed
His monarch's freshened face and went out in
The deep blue dusk of sunset, all his heart
A mass of pain and hatred. All night he writhed,
Until day came and night's black cloak was torn.   210

When this malign man woke he made his way
To Afrasyab; the court was cleared of strangers—
The two sat down, discussing various matters,
Till Garsivaz said, 'O my king, the habits,
The behavior of prince Seyavash have changed.
A messenger came frequently to him,
In secret, from Kavus and messages
Have come from China and Byzantium;
He drinks Kavus's health; a massive army's
220   Collected round him—there will come the day
When he will give your royal soul no rest.
If Tur had not been discontented with
The portion of the world his father gave him,
He'd not have wronged Iraj[69]—but now these lands,
Irreconcilable as fire and water,
Feel hatred for each other in their hearts.
And you insanely hope to make them one?
You might as well attempt to cage the winds!
If I'd have kept this evil hidden from you,
230   Throughout the world my name would be dishonored.'
The king's heart grieved at this and, fearing Fate's
Fell course, he said, 'It's your blood's kinship with me
That's prompted you and been your guide; we must
For three days think this matter through and take
The best advice. If wisdom should confirm this,
I'll say what remedy you'll have to look for.'
When on the fourth day Garsivaz arrived
At court, his ceremonial crown in place,
His sword-belt tightly buckled, Afrasyab
240   Summoned him to his side and talked at length
About the business of prince Seyavash.
He said, 'How you remind me of Pashang!
What have I in the world that I can trust,
That's in my hands, but you? I must disclose
My secrets, all of them, to you! Look deeply,
See what you think. That evil dream I had
Which so upset me, it confused my mind
To some extent—so that I made no move

To fight with Seyavash and no harm came
To me from him. When he gave up the throne,   250
Wisdom the warp he wove and me the weft!
He never turned his head from anything
I ordered and he benefited greatly
From all I did for him—I handed him
A province and my wealth; I never mentioned
The troubles I'd endured on his behalf.
And then I made a blood alliance with him,
Forswore all thoughts of vengeance on Iran,
I gave him both my treasure and my child,
As dear as is the sight of these two eyes   260
And, if now after all this kindness, all
These different sorrows, after sacrificing
My country, crown and wealth to him, if now
I were to be suspicious of this man,
The world would fill with murmurings against me.
I've no excuse to harm him—if the least
Harm came to him from me, I'd be condemned
By all the country's nobles, in the world
I'd be a byword for bad faith. Neither God
Nor earthly rulers would approve of me.   270
A lion has sharper teeth than any beast
And fears no swords, but if its cub is hurt
It makes a safe asylum for it deep
In the meadows; were I to persecute
This innocent would God Who rules the sun
And moon look kindly on me?[70] Well, I see
No other course but to recall him to
Our court and then dismiss him to his father—
In this way, if he wants the power a throne
And royal signet-ring confer, he'll take   280
His quarrel elsewhere and this land won't be
The loser by it.' Garsivaz replied,
'My lord, don't treat such weighty matters lightly;
If he leaves here and gets back to Iran,
Our country will be utterly destroyed;
A stranger welcomed to your family

Knows all your secrets, great and small; if you
Now try to separate yourself from him,
He'll guide here who knows what insanity
290   And be another enemy to rub
Salt in our wounds. A wise man once remarked
That when a storm has burst forth from your house
You'll find no way to stop it in its course
And Fate will not relent although you must.
This Seyavash knows all of your affairs
As well as everything you've said—you'll not
See anything from him but pain and grief,
The dissipation of your tribe, your name
And all your wealth. Aren't you aware that one
300   Who brings a leopard up sees nothing from
His charge but pain and strife?' When Afrasyab
Considered Garsivaz's words they all
Seemed true to him—then he regretted what
He'd thought and done, his former policy
Seemed wrong to him, and he replied, 'I can't
See any good in this, its end and its
Beginning seem disastrous. But let's wait
Until the turning heavens show their will
In the affair—in every matter haste
310   Is worse than waiting, so we'll let the sun
Rise high into the sky awhile; I'll watch
To see God's purposes, to see on whom
The lamp of heaven shines. If I recall
Him to this court, I'll sound his secrets out
In conversation—and I'm sure that I'm
Sufficiently alert to be his match.
I'll see how things turn out; if it becomes
Apparent that he's crooked, that I've no choice
Except to be hard-hearted, then no one is
320   To blame—the punishment of evil must
Be evil too, and there's an end of it.'
And Garsivaz, who longed to stir up trouble,
Answered, 'My king, whose words are wise, whose heart's

Discerning, were this Seyavash to come
To court with all his pomp and power, his strength
And his God-given might, his mace and sword—
Were he to come here with his army, then
The sun and moon would shine no more for you.
This Seyavash is not the man the king
Once saw, he lifts his crown above the heavens,   330
And in the same way you'd not recognize
Your Farigis, she seems beyond the needs
Of earthly life. Your troops will all defect
To Seyavash, and with no flock there can't
Be any shepherd. [71] When an army's seen
A king like him—his generosity,
His wisdom and his face as handsome as
The moon itself—can you then say to him,
"Be my obedient slave, content to live
In lowliness on what I choose to hand you"?   340
No one has ever seen an elephant
Select a lion as its mate, or fire
That roars above while water flows below.
If someone takes a lion-cub that's still
Not tasted milk and wraps it in silk cloth,
When it grows up it will revert to what
Its nature is, and it won't even fear
The threat of some wild elephant's attack.'
Then Afrasyab felt trapped by what he'd heard,
He grew despondent, sunk in anxious thoughts,   350
But still delay seemed preferable to haste,
The patient stone outlasts all enmity
And no one praises empty-headed rashness.
A wise man once remarked about such matters,
'If wind did not whirl wildly here and there,
It would have substance and a lasting strength.'
A rash, light-headed man lacks staying power,
Although his body might be cypress-tall.
They parted then, both gnawed by discontent;
Their lips were filled with murmurings, their hearts   360

With brooding on revenge for ancient wrongs.
Now Garsivaz, malignant and malicious,
Came to the king repeatedly; he mixed
The colors of malevolence and turned
The Turkish monarch's heart against the prince
Until the time came when the king was filled
With pain and hatred. One day, having cleared
The court of strangers, Afrasyab discussed
In detail all the problems of the prince
370   With Garsivaz, then said, 'You'll have to go
To him, don't stay there as his guest too long
But ask him how things are and say from me,
"You've no desire to leave this pleasant place,
It seems, and see your friends—but here hearts long
For you; come, visit us with Farigis,
I need to see you, to have contact with
Your excellent intelligence again.
There's hunting in our hills, our emerald cups
Hold wine and milk. Let's spend a little time
380   In happiness together—when once again
You want to see your city, you can leave
Us cheerfully with music sounding round you.
Why is it wrong to drink your wine with me?" '

So cunning Garsivaz, whose head was filled
With wiles, his heart with hate, prepared to leave.
When he was near to Seyavash's city
He chose a glib, well-practiced talker from
Among his troops and said to him, 'Go now,
And say to Seyavash, "O nobly born
390   Of an ambitious king, I beg you by
Turan's great monarch's head and soul and by
The glory and the crown of king Kavus
That you do not, for me, bestir yourself
Or leave the throne to travel on the roads
To welcome me! For by your grace and glory,
Your fortune and your birth, your crown and throne,

You are too great to leave the royal couch—
Even the winds should gird themselves to serve you!" '72
The messenger reached Seyavash's court
And kissed the ground as he caught sight of him.   400
When he'd repeated Garsivaz's message
Prince Seyavash was saddened and withdrew
Into a private chamber where he thought
At length about the matter. To himself
He said, 'There is some secret hidden here;
I wonder what my good friend Garsivaz
Has said about me in the other court.'
When Garsivaz arrived in this new city
The prince went from the palace to the street
To welcome him; he questioned him about   410
His journey, and the king's affairs, the troops,
The crown and throne. The message from the king
Was handed over and delighted him—
He said in answer to it, 'For his sake
I'd outface swords of steel; my preparations
Are as good as made already and I'll link
My reins with yours—we'll travel back together!
But first for three days, in this gold pavilion,
Let's rest at ease and give ourselves to wine;
The world is fleeting, full of pain and sorrow,   420
Alas for him who spends his little life
In sadness!' But when the prince's prudent words
Were heard by the malignant Garsivaz
He writhed within and in his heart he said,
'If Seyavash, with his sagacious mind
And lion-like nobility, should now
Come back with me to Afrasyab, my plans
Will all be trampled underfoot—my words
Will lose their luster and the king will see
My scheming as a lie. I must work out   430
Some other course now and pervert the heart
Of Seyavash into an evil road.'
He stood awhile in silence and his eyes

Were fixed on Seyavash's face; then from
His eyes the sallow tears flowed down, and with
These tears he put his strategy to work.
When Seyavash saw that his face was wet
Like one whom sympathy has moved to tears,
He gently said to him, 'What's this, my brother?
440   Is it a sorrow you can talk about?
If some act of the Turkish king has wet
Your eyes with grief, I'll go there with you now
And fight against Turan's king and his troops
Until I know why he's oppressing you
And thinks of you as his inferior.
Or if some enemy's appeared before you,
Someone's it's right to guard against and fear,
Whatever happens I will help you, and when
You fight against him I'll be your support.
450   Or is it that your reputation's dimmed
With Afrasyab, or that some slanderer
Is by his lies outclimbing you at court?'
And the illustrious Garsivaz replied,
'There's no dispute between the king and me
And I'm not worried about enemies—
My wealth and courage are an adequate
Resource to deal with them. My heart was filled
With thoughts of race and I remembered those
True ancient stories we all know. The first
460   From whom our evil came was Tur—the man
Abandoned by God's gift of Royal Glory;[73]
You've heard how his malevolence attacked
The self-effacing, innocent Iraj—
From that first murder to the present time
Of Afrasyab Iran has been like fire,
Turan like water, and the two won't mix—
They've never done so—in one place since then;
Both broke the bonds of wisdom and advice.
The present Turkish king is worse than Tur,
470   And wait, his ox has not been skinned as yet![74]
No doubt you're ignorant of his cruel nature,

But watch awhile and time will show his evil.
Look first at how he dealt with Aghriras[75]
Whom wildly, with his own hands, he destroyed;
He was his brother, from the same womb, sired
By the same father, and yet he killed this wise
And guiltless man; and then how many since,
How many famous, guiltless men have met
Destruction at his hands! Now, above all,
My chief anxiety's for you, that you   480
Should live unharmed and with your wits about you.
Since you have come into our territories
No man's been hurt by you, you've always acted
With manly chivalry and righteousness,
Making the world more beautiful with wisdom.
But Ahriman who sunders hearts has turned
Our king's intemperately against you and now
His heart is filled with pain and hate for you—
I don't know what God wills in all of this
But you know I feel only friendship for you,   490
That I'll support you come what may of good
Or ill. You mustn't think tomorrow that
I knew about this feud and never warned you.'
But Seyavash replied, 'Don't brood on this;
The world's Creator, God, is my support,
And Afrasyab has never given me
Cause to believe he'd turn my day to night.
If in his heart he'd been annoyed with me,
He wouldn't have exalted me above
All others—given me a province, crown   500
And royal throne, these wide estates, his child,
His troops and wealth. But now I'll go with you
To court and make king Afrasyab's dark moon
Blaze brightly once again. Wherever truth
Shines out, the luster of a lie is dimmed.
I'll show my heart to Afrasyab, and it
Will shine more brightly than the sun in heaven.
Be happy in your heart, avoid suspicion;
That man the evil dragon's breath does not

510   Engulf can never not be in God's care.'[76]
    But Garsivaz said, 'My kind lord, don't think
    That Afrasyab is still the man you saw;
    And when the turning heavens cloud and frown
    A wise man knows what storms will lift above
    The curved horizon—but with all your knowledge,
    The shrewdness of your heart, your cypress-stature,
    Your noble thoughts, you still can't tell true kindness
    From opportune pretence. May bad luck gain
    No hold on you, but he's bewitched you by
520   His tricks and sewn the eyes of wisdom up
    With sorcery. When first he lured you on
    By making you his son-in-law, your joy
    Was foolish; next, when he got rid of you
    And made a feast for you before the nobles,
    He did it in the hopes that you would take
    Some unbecoming liberty, so that
    The world would fill with murmurings against you.
    You're not a greater man than Aghriras
    Or closer to the king than him, and he
530   Was—to the horror of the army—slashed
    In two; and by the king's own dagger. Look,
    His hidden purposes are plain to you now;
    Know what they are, don't trust the ties of blood.
    I've told you all my heart's thoughts, what I know
    And what I've learnt of this vindictive king—
    I've listed them for you so that they're plain
    As is the shining sun. You left your father
    In Iran, and in Turan you've built a city,
    Given your heart to this king's glozing words
540   And sympathized with all his sorrows, but
    The tree you've planted is an evil one—
    Its fruits are poison and its roots are bitter
    As the colocynth.' He spoke, his eyes were wet
    With sallow tears, his heart was filled with cunning,
    Cold sighs escaped his lips. And Seyavash
    Stared wildly at him, tears coursing down his cheeks,
    While he recalled misfortune would be his

And that the heavens would not look kindly on him;
Few days were left to him, and he would die
While still a youth. His heart was filled with pain,   550
His cheeks grew sallow, sorrow filled his heart,
Cold sighs escaped his lips. He said to him,
'However I reflect on what I've done,
I can't see I deserve such punishment;
No one has heard of any evil act
Or speech by me; and if my hand has been
Too open with his wealth, my heart is hurt
By his annoyance. Even so, although
It might endanger me, I'll not ignore
His will or his commands. I'll go to him   560
Immediately without my troops and try
To find out why the king's upset with me.'
But the ambitious Garsivaz replied,
'You shouldn't go to him; you shouldn't step
Into the fire, or trust to ocean waves;
You're rushing into danger pointlessly
And lulling your good luck to sleep. I'll be
Sufficient intermediary and throw
Cold water on these flames. You'll have to write
A letter to him, plainly setting out   570
The good and evil of the situation.
Now if I see he's free from thoughts of vengeance
And that good Fortune smiles, I'll send a horseman
To you, and make your dark thoughts bright again.
I trust in God Who made the world, Who knows
What's open and what's hidden, and I hope
Our king will turn to righteousness and shun
All fraud and crooked dealing. If I find,
However, that his mind is darkened still,
I'll get a message to you straight away   580
And you should take the necessary steps
At once—make no delay in seeking safety;
Ride from this country to some other land,
There are illustrious kings and nobles near—
From here to China's not more than a hundred

And twenty parasangs, and to Iran's
Three hundred and thirty. There everyone's
Your friend, your servant, sympathetic to
Your cause, and there your father longs to see you—
590   The world is his there and belongs to you.
Write lengthy letters now to everyone,
Prepare to leave and waste no time about it.'
And Seyavash believed the things he said;
His cunning slept, and he replied, 'I'll do
As you've suggested, I won't deviate
From your advice; go to the king and plead
My cause. Seek righteousness, and be my guide.'

SEYAVASH WRITES A LETTER TO AFRASYAB

A learned scribe was called and Seyavash
Dictated pregnant words to him. He first
Repaid the debt of wisdom in his soul,
Invoking God and praising wisdom's ways;
He called down blessings on the Turkish king
And said, 'Victorious and fortunate
Great king, may no time ever dawn when you
Are but a memory! You've summoned me
And happily I hear your summons now
10   (So may you sit surrounded by the wise!),
And Farigis you've summoned too, and shown
The love and loyalty within your heart.
But now our Farigis is sick, her lips
Will not touch food, she lacks the strength to walk;
When she is well she'll come to you, prepared
To sacrifice her life for yours, for now
The pain she's suffering's my excuse—
My secret's my anxiety for her.'
He sealed the note and handed it at once
20   To the malignant Garsivaz, who asked
For three fleet horses; day and night he rode
And on the fourth day reached the great king's court,
His mind intent on evil and his lips

All lies. When Afrasyab saw his distress
And haste, he questioned him at length and said,
'Why have you come so quickly, covering such
A massive distance in so short a time?'
He answered, 'When the face of things is darkened,
It does not do to put one's trust in Fortune;
This Seyavash showed no respect to me
Or anyone—he didn't travel out   *told him not to*   30
To welcome me, or listen to my greetings,
Or read your letter. Then he made me kneel
Before his throne; the door of his affection
Was closed against me. Constantly he gets
New letters from Iran; his territories
Resound each day with armies come from China
And from Byzantium. If you delay
In dealing with this man, your fist will close
On wind and nothing more. If you hold back
From fighting him, his valor will ensure   40
He'll get both countries in his grasp; if he
Should lead his army to Iran, who'd dare
To challenge him to fight? I'm warning you
Of what I've witnessed with these eyes—now writhe
In this affair that you yourself created.'
When Afrasyab heard this the ancient days
And all their hatred were renewed for him—
In fury he made no reply; his heart
Was filled with fire, his head seemed wild as wind.
He gave his orders that the fifes and trumpets,   50
The cymbals and the Indian chimes be sounded,
And set out for the court of Seyavash
Accompanied by his proud and warlike nobles.

Now while the cunning Garsivaz strained in
The stirrups, Seyavash went trembling to
The women's quarters of his palace, pain
In his heart, his cheeks grown pallid. Farigis
Addressed him, 'O my hero, lion-clawed,
What's happened?—Your complexion's grown so pale!'   60

He answered her, 'My lovely Farigis,
My honor's been destroyed here in Turan!
The way that Garsivaz described my life
It's almost come full circle.' Farigis
Clutched at her curls and with her nails she scored
The roses of her face. She tore her hair
And wept to think what Afrasyab would say
And do. She cried, 'My noble lord, where can
You turn now? Tell me everything, be quick!
70   Your father's still enraged with you, and you
Can't even think of turning to Iran;
Byzantium's too far to fly to—you
Won't run away to China out of shame.
Who in the world can you now ask for refuge?
Your only refuge is the God Who rules
The sun and moon. May months, may years of pain
Destroy the soul of him who's slandered you.
He said, 'But Garsivaz will soon return
And bring me greetings from the king again.'
80   Then on the fourth night, Seyavash asleep
Within the arms of lovely Farigis
Trembled and started up, and gave a scream
Wild as a maddened elephant's; his wife
Still clung to him and, moved by love, she said,
'My lord, what is it?' But he screamed again—
They lit the lamps and burnt in front of him
Sweet ambergris and aloes wood. She asked,
'My noble prince, what was the dream you saw?'
And to the daughter of king Afrasyab
90   Prince Seyavash replied, 'Keep your lips closed;
Tell no one of the dream I've seen; my love,
Whose body's like a silver cypress tree,
I dreamt I saw a mighty river flowing—
And on the other side a mountain all
Of flame; the shore was held by warriors
With spears. On one side flaming fire spread out
And burnt the city I've called Seyavashkard.
Here fire, there water, while before me stood

The army's elephants and Afrasyab.
He glared at me, his face was filled with frowns,   100
And with his breath he blew the scorching fire.'
But Farigis said, 'This can only mean
That everything will turn out for the best;
Now rest, my lord, lie down and sleep awhile.'

But Seyavash called all his army to him
And for a long time, in his audience chamber,
He gave instructions and prepared for war;
He sat, a dagger in his hand, and sent
Out scouts to mount guard on the road to Gang.
Two watches of dark night had passed when they   110
Returned from spying in the wastelands and said,
'A mighty army led by Afrasyab's
Apparent in the distance, pressing forward.'
And then a messenger from Garsivaz
Appeared, saying, 'Prepare to save your skin,
My words had no effect, and from this fire
I see black smoke come billowing; decide
Now what you ought to do, and where your troops
Will have to be deployed.' Still Seyavash
Was unsuspecting and believed his words.   120
Queen Farigis said, 'Wisest prince, take no
Account of us, have no faith in Turan
But saddle some quick-footed horse and leave—
I want you living, now and in the future,
Save your own head and wait for no one here!'
But Seyavash replied, 'My dream's come true;
My glory's darkened now and life for me
Draws to its end; sorrow and pain and grief
Are mine, as is the turning heaven's way
Which shows now joy, now wretchedness; and if   130
My palace dome should touch the sphere of Saturn,
The poison of this world must still be tasted.
If for a thousand and two hundred years
We live, the black dust is our home at last—
And in this night no wise man hopes to find

The brightness of the day. You're five months pregnant;
If you're delivered safely, if the fruit
Maturing on the tree should grow to ripeness,
You'll give birth to a glorious prince; see that
140   You name him Kay Khosrow—and in the pains
You bear in bearing him find peace. Thus turns
The whirling circle of the heavens, and men
Will never see this ancient dwelling change.
And now, through Afrasyab's commands, my dark
Luck sinks to sleep. They'll hack my guiltless head off
And in my body's blood they'll soak my crown;
I'll find no coffin, grave or shroud, and of
The company who's there not one will weep;
My final resting place will be Turan.
150   This ancient world is like a lion's maw;
Such is the fate the heavens will bring to me,
No happiness is promised me, or kindness,
But from the shining sun to darkest earth
No being can escape the will of God.
And you, humiliated, with your head
And body naked, will be dragged along
The highway by the king's own guards; Piran
The great commander will arrive at court
And beg you from your father, offering refuge
160   To your innocence. He'll take you, weeping, wailing,
To his ancestral palace. From Iran
A savior who's been sent by God will come,
And quickly, secretly, he'll lead your son
And you to where the Oxus marks the border.
They'll place your son upon the royal throne
And he will rule the birds in heaven, the fish
Within the depths. The times will then be torn
With tumult, Kay Khosrow will plunge the world
In war, an army from Iran will come,
170   Intent on vengeance—terror will spread throughout
This land from end to end, and Rostam's horse,
Great Rakhsh, will tread this soil beneath its hooves;
Then no one in Turan will be thought human—

In vengeance for my death, from that day on
Until the resurrection comes, you'll see
Sharp swords and maces here and nothing else.
Brood on these words I say within your heart;
Your body now must bid farewell to peace
And luxury.' When Seyavash had told
His wife his grief she clung to him and wept,   180
And all his face was bathed in desperate tears.
He went then to the stables where they stalled
His Arab horses and picked out black Behzad,
Who on the battlefield outran the wind,
And, lifting off the halter, took its head
Within his arms and, weeping, whispered in
Its ear the secrets of his heart. He said,
'Be wary of all men till Kay Khosrow
Shall come here to avenge my death, it's he
Who must replace the bridle on your head   190
Then bid farewell for ever to this stable
And bear the hero out to war and vengeance.'
He hamstrung all the other horses, wild
As fire that burns through reeds, and with his warriors
Turned towards Iran, his face obscured by tears.

But after half a parasang he found
King Afrasyab confronting him, and saw
His troops in battle-armour, armed with swords
And helmeted. And as he buckled on
His armor Seyavash said in his heart,   200
'The words of Garsivaz were true, and how
Could what he said be hidden or denied?'
He feared now for his life; the two sides watched
Each other's ranks—before there'd been no hate
For one another in their hearts. From fear
Of Seyavash the Turkish horsemen paused
And hung back, hesitating. Seyavash
Called out to Afrasyab, 'Great king, possessed
Of might and glory, why have you come here
Accompanied by your troops, intent on war?   210

Why should you kill me, since I'm innocent?
You'll set at odds the armies of two countries
And fill this time and territory with curses.'
But Garsivaz impatiently broke in,
'How can you say such worthless things!
If you're so innocent, why have you come before
The king in armor? This is not the way
To welcome us, and spears and shields are not

220   Fit presents for a king!' Then Seyavash
Knew Garsivaz had been behind it all
And that the king's rage was because of him.
The sun had risen now; when Afrasyab
Heard Garsivaz's words he told his Turks,
'Now soak this plain in blood to such a depth
That you can set a ship afloat on it.'
There were a thousand Persian warriors there,
All famous fighters fit for war—they formed
Their battle order then, prepared for bloodshed;

230   All fought with Seyavash, they did not see
How cunning or delay could help them now.
'If they're to slaughter us,' they cried, 'it won't
Be they alone who sup on blood, but let
Them understand what war with Persians means,
And not consider it contemptible!'
But Seyavash said, 'There's no wisdom here,
This war has neither rhyme nor reason to it;
But what have sages said?—That courage is
No use against an evil star. If now

240   The turning heavens will that I shall die,
Destroyed by evil men, no courage can
Avail me, since no man can fight with God.'
That day disaster struck and all were killed.
The prince was wounded by a lance and arrows
And tumbled headlong from his sable horse;
Still crawling in the dust he clutched his spear,
But Gerui wrenched both his hands behind
His back and tied them tight, immovable
As stone; they slung a halter round his neck,

Blood stained the roses of this young man's cheeks
Whose eyes had never seen a day like this.   250
With troops surrounding him on every side,
They marched to Seyavashkard. When they arrived[77]
The Turks' king, Afrasyab, called, 'Drag him to
The roadside there and with a dagger hack
His head off on the hard ground where no plants
Can grow; get on with it—don't be afraid—
And spill his blood upon the burning earth!'
But with one voice the army cried, 'O king,
What crimes can you accuse him of? Why kill
A man for whom the crown and ivory throne   260
Themselves will weep? Wise king, the head that's worn
A crown should not be cut off in this way;
Now, in the days of your prosperity,
Don't plant the tree which one day will produce
A poisoned crop.' Malignant Garsivaz,
Who, in his folly, was the friend of those
Who murdered men, was there and longed to shed
The blood of Seyavash because he'd been
Humiliated by him on the field
Of battle. But Pilsom, Piran's young brother   270
A wise, accomplished youth, and noble as
Piran himself—was there as well and said
To Afrasyab, 'The fruit of what you're now
About to plant will be harsh pain and sorrow;
I've heard from those who know—and wisdom would
Agree with this—that he who is not rash
Has little to regret; that reason is a balm
To soothe the angry heart; that haste and evil
Belong to Ahriman, that they torment
The soul with pangs of guilt, the flesh with pain.   280
I cannot see how it is right that you
Should recklessly behead your subject here;
Keep him in chains till time will show what's best,
And when the wind of wisdom's touched your heart
Then that will be the time for execution.
Have chains brought, and forget this haste since haste

Can only bring regret. If you cut off
This guiltless prince's head, Kavus and Rostam
Are ready for revenge—his father is
290   Kavus and Rostam raised the boy—and you
Will live to rue the day you did this when
Such warriors as Gudarz and Giv, Borzin
And Tus, strap war-drums on their elephants.
Rostam, who's blessed with elephantine strength,
In whose eyes armies are beneath contempt,
And Fariborz, a roaring lion in battle,
Kavus's son, whom no one's ever seen
To tire of war, will both bind on their belts
For vengeance—all the steppe will overflow
300   With warriors, and neither I nor any of
My kin, nor any of this company
Will have the strength to stand against their onslaught.
At dawn Piran will come, and may the king
Hear his advice; there's no necessity
For you to end the matter here and now;
Delay, don't spread revenge throughout the world!'
But Garsivaz said, 'Wisest king, don't change
Your mind because of young men's words. The plains
Are filled with vultures because of these same
310   Persians, and if you fear to take revenge
This is sufficient cause! And isn't all
The evil you have done enough without
Compounding it by taking bad advice?
If Seyavash cries out, you'll see this land
Filled with the swords of China and of Rome.
You've chopped the snake's tail off and crushed its head.
You want to wrap its body in brocade?
If now you spare his life, I'll quit your court
And live my life out fearfully in some
320   Wild jungle clearing.' Damur and Gerui
Came full of plausible and twisted words
Before the Turkish king and said, 'Don't fret
Yourself about the blood of Seyavash—
It's wrong to hold back when there's work to do;

Take Garsivaz's good advice, and rid
The world of him since he's your enemy.
You've laid a trap and snared him, there will be
An outcry from Iran in any case.
We mustn't keep him prisoner now, but act
And break the hearts of those who slander us!   330
You've slaughtered all his troops, consider how
This prince will think of you. If from the first
You hadn't harmed them, then a little water
Would wash away the fault—but now it's best
That no one in the world know what has happened.'
The king replied to them, 'I've seen, myself,
No fault in him, although astrologers
Have said that in the end he'd harm this land;
If I now shed his blood, the dust of armies
Intent on vengeance will obscure Iran;   340
But freeing him is worse than killing him,
And killing him for me is pain and sorrow;
My ruin will be the ruin of Turan
And sorrow, grief and slavery threaten us.
But neither wise nor evil men know what
The turning heavens hold in store for them.'
When Farigis learnt this she clawed her cheeks
And gave herself to grief; on foot she came
Before the king, her moon-like cheeks blood-smeared
She fell before her father, heaping her hair   350
With dust, wailing and filled with dread and pain;
She cried, 'Great king why will you overwhelm
Me with such misery? Why have you let
Your heart be cheated?—From the height of power
You cannot see the depths beneath your gaze;
The Lord Who rules the sun and moon cannot
Approve of one who kills a guiltless prince.
When Seyavash forsook Iran it was
To you—of all the world—that he paid homage,
Angering his father for your sake, renouncing   360
His crown and throne and might; he came to you
For refuge and support! What new act have

You seen from him? Who's made you change your mind?
The man who means to keep his crown and throne
Does not behead a king who wears a crown!
And I am innocent, do not destroy me—
The world is fleeting, and as insubstantial
As a breath of wind; it flings a guiltless man
Into a dungeon, lifts another up
370   To glory and a throne, but finally
The star that rules our lives lays both of them
Within the grave's grip and beneath the dust.
You've heard the fate Zahhak the Arab tyrant
Suffered at Faridun the Warrior's hands—
The same that Salm and vicious Tur had dealt
To them by Manuchehr, that mighty king;[78]
Kavus's court is now the home of Zal
And of his fierce vindictive son Rostam,
At whom the whole world trembles, whom Turan
380   Has not the strength to fight; and there's Bahram
And Zangeh, Shavran's son, who doesn't give
A thought to warrior's weapons ranged against him;
There's Giv too, fear of whom when combat threatens
Will make a leopard slink off like a fox.
You're planting in the earth a tree whose leaves
Are blood, whose fruit is poisonous; the streams
Will darken cursing Afrasyab and weep
With grief for Seyavash. It is yourself
Whom you'll destroy and all too often you'll
390   Recall these words of mine. This is no hunt
For onager, it's not young deer you're frightening—
It is a king you're toppling from his throne,
And you had best consider carefully
What you're about; don't throw this realm, Turan,
Thoughtlessly to the winds, you must not make
Today an evil day that you'll regret.'
She spoke and seeing Seyavash's face
Clawed her two cheeks and sobbed aloud; the king's
Heart bled for her, but anger sealed the eyes
400   Of wisdom and he said, 'Get out and don't

Come back; what do you know of my opinion
Of this evil?' There was a room inside
The palace Farigis knew nothing of,
And there they threw her and secured the door.

SEYAVASH IS KILLED

Then Garsivaz looked straight at Gerui,
Cruel Gerui, who turned his face aside
And stood in front of Seyavash, devoid
Of chivalry and shame.[79] King Afrasyab
Commanded them to lead off Seyavash,
The silent prince who had no hatred in him.
He said, 'Cut off his head, away from all
His friends and comrades, sever it with one
Quick stroke, and let the flocking vultures be
His body's shroud. But see the ground does not   10
Absorb the blood of Seyavash since, if
It does, the plant of vengeance will spring up.'
The murderous sentries dragged him, stumbling, away,
And Seyavash cried out to God, 'O Thou
Who art above vicissitudes of Fate,
Bring forth a sapling from my seed, a man
Who'll be a shining sun to all my people,
Who'll wreak revenge on these my enemies,
And in his realm renew the ancient ways.'
Pilsom came after him, his eyes awash   20
With desperate tears, his heart with grief. To him
Prince Seyavash said, 'Go, I wish you well—
May Fortune always weave its threads with yours;
And give Piran my greetings, say to him,
"The world has changed, and this is not what I
Had hoped for from Piran; his words were like
A wind before which like a willow I
Bowed down; he said that when misfortune came
He'd be my friend, a pasture for my foraging,
That with a hundred thousand infantry   30

And armored cavalry he'd come. But now
I'm hurried, stumbling and humiliated,
In front of Garsivaz, my soul all darkness—
And see no friend who's come to weep for me." '
When they'd gone on beyond the town and army
They dragged him to the desert; Gerui,
Intent on murder, took a glittering dagger
From Garsivaz; they threw the mammoth prince
Down in the dust and Gerui, who felt
40   No shame or fear, brought out a golden bowl
To catch the blood and hacked the head off from
The silver cypress of the prince's body.
He took the bowl where Afrasyab had ordered
And emptied it. A wind of black thick dust
Sprang up, obscuring all the sun and moon,
And men could not make out each other's faces;
They fell to cursing Gerui—for when
The sun was separated from the cypress,
The king's head sank into an endless sleep
50   And never moved and never woke again;
And since the throne and battlefield have lost
Their king, may there be neither sun nor cypress![80]

I search to right and left, on every side,
And see no sense, no head or tail, in how
This earth goes—since one man does evil deeds
And luck is his, the world is like his slave,
While one who never acts unrighteously
Withers away in wretchedness. But keep
Your distance from the sorrow of this world
60   And do not let it grieve your heart and soul.

Wailing went up from Seyavash's palace—
The world was filled with tumult on account
Of Garsivaz; the lovely women of
His household tore their curls and clawed their cheeks,
Helpless with grief; the slaves' hair hung disheveled—
Queen Farigis cut off her tresses' long

Dark noose and twisted it about her waist,
And with her hennaed nails she scored her cheeks;
Weeping, she cursed the soul of Afrasyab,
And when her cries and curses reached the king   70
He said to evil-minded Garsivaz,
'Bring her here—into the open—have the guards
Hale her by the hair and strip her in the street,
And have them beat her till she voids this seed
Of vengeance in Turan, since I'll not let
A branch or leaf or crown or throne spring from
The root of this tree Seyavash.' Then all
The nobles who were there condemned the king
And one by one declared they'd never heard
Of such a sentence ordered by a king   80
Or minister or warrior. Pilsom,
Seared in his soul, came with his cheeks all wet
To Farshidvard and to Lahhak and told
Them what the king had ordered, adding, 'Hell
Is better than the realm of Afrasyab,
There'll be no rest or sleep within these borders—
Let's hurry to Piran, and to relieve
The pain and sorrow that these prisoners suffer.'
They saddled three good horses and the earth
Sped by beneath them till they reached Piran,   90
Their faces wet as clouds in spring with blood
And tears. At once they went through what had happened,
And all the evils Fortune had devised;
'A lamentation's risen in the world
Beyond what any man has seen before—
They bound the hands of Seyavash as hard
As stone and placed a halter round his neck,
They dragged him stumbling, weeping, to Gerui
And, taking no account of anyone,
They flung his mammoth body to the ground;   100
When Gerui had placed a bowl before
The prince, he twisted up the victim's neck
As if he were a sheep and hacked his head
Off from his body and let him lie there like

A noble cypress toppled to the ground.
The whole town wept and wailed for him, the eyes
Of everyone were filled with tears like dew.'
And when Piran had heard their words he fell
Down from his throne as if incapable,
Then ripped his clothes, tore at his hair, heaped dust
Upon his head. Pilsom said, 'Come quickly now,
For pain is piled on pain and greater grief
Is threatened, they will kill queen Farigis—
Don't turn your back on her distress; the guards
Have dragged her to the king's court by her hair,
The evil Afrasyab has made her world
A vale of tears, and what's most horrible
Is that he'll have her hacked in half—this act
Will utterly destroy his sovereignty,
No man will ever call him king again.'
The champion brought ten[81] horses from his stable,
All young but tried and tested mounts, and he,
The warrior Ruin and Farshidvard
Sent up the road's dust in their haste. It took
Two days and nights for them to reach the court;
Piran saw men whose trade was cruelty crowded
About the gateway, and Farigis, as if
Insensible, dragged forward by the guards,
Their sharp swords ready in their fists.[82] The court
Rang with a tumult like the Day of Judgment
As like the wind Piran arrived, and all
Who'd any wisdom there rejoiced to see him.
When Farigis saw that Piran had come
Her face was bathed in desperate tears, and she
Cried out, 'Look at the evil that you've done.[83]
Why have you wildly flung me to the flames?'
Piran fell from his horse, he tore his clothes
In grief, gave orders that the guards hold back
A moment from the task that they'd been given,
And ran to Afrasyab, his heart in pain,
Tears welling in his eyes, and said, 'O king,
Live prosperously, with an enlightened soul!

110

120

130

140

What evil's come to you, my generous lord,
Who's brought this day of foul desires to you?
How has a devil overthrown your heart
And rendered you so shameless before God?
You've killed the guiltless Seyavash and hurled
His noble name and glory in the dust;
When news of this foul act has reached Iran,
When they learn that the gracious cypress tree   150
Is withered now and dead, how many lords
Of Persia will lead out their armies here
Intent on war and vengeance! For a while
The world was undisturbed by crime—the way
Of God was plain—but some deceitful devil
Has sprung from hell and worked its evil on
The Turkish monarch's heart. And rightly should
That Ahriman who's turned aside your soul
To wicked ways be cursed! You will regret
This act for endless days; how long you'll writhe   160
In sorrow and in anguish over this!
I don't know whose foul words have prompted this
Or what the world's Creator means by it—
But like a lunatic you've risen up
And wildly set your hand to evil acts.
And now you're quit of Seyavash you turn
Against your wretched child, your flesh and blood;
Your Farigis has no desire for power,
For royal glory, or a crown or throne.
Don't act against your child, within whose womb   170
A baby's growing, in such a way that you'll
Become contemptible throughout the world
While you're alive you'll be condemned and cursed,
And when life's over hell will be your fate.
But it will brighten my dark soul if you
Will send her to my palace; if her child's
The reason why you're worried, that's a small
And unimportant matter—wait until
It's born. I'll bring it to you then and you
Can do your worst with it.' He answered him,   180

'Well, do as you suggest with her; you've made
Me feel reluctant now to shed her blood.'
Piran rejoiced at this; the great commander
Was freed from his anxiety and pain.
He went back to the gates, took Farigis,
And paid the guards who'd held her handsomely.
He took her to Khotan, unhurt, while all
The court and company applauded him.
Once back in his own palace he addressed
190   Golshahr, 'This lovely girl must be concealed,
Keep her in safety and look after her.'
And so the days passed by, and Farigis,
Whose beauty lit the world, grew heavier.

THE BIRTH OF KING KAY KHOSROW

One pitch-dark, moonless night while birds, wild beasts
And cattle slept, Piran saw in a dream
A candle flame lit from the sun; within
The flame stood Seyavash and in his hand
He held his sword; he called out in a loud voice,
'This is no time for rest! Come, rouse yourself
From pleasant sleep; consider how the world
Moves onward to its end, and how new customs,
New festivals begin; tonight will be
10   The feast that marks the birth of Kay Khosrow.'
Piran woke trembling from his welcome dream,
Golshahr as splendid as the sun sprang up
From sleep; her husband said to her, 'Go now,
Discreetly visit Farigis; I dreamt
Of Seyavash, he shone more brightly than
The sun in heaven and said to me, "How long
Will you sleep here? Come, join the festival
That celebrates the birth of Kay Khosrow."
Golshahr went to the moonlike beauty's side
20   And saw that she had borne a son, a king,
And lightly, quickly hurried back—the world

Was filled immediately with acclamations
As in her happiness she told Piran,
'The sun and moon have married—hurry now
And see the miracle that is their child,
The greatness and the will of God; you'll say
This baby's born to wear a crown—or for
The armor, helmet, plunder of a warrior.'
The army's leader came to see the prince
And brought him presents, praising him profusely—   30
His stature, chest and shoulders seemed as if
He were a boy already one year old;
Piran's eyes filled with tears for Seyavash;
He cursed king Afrasyab and to the nobles
Who were assembled there he said, 'Though he
Destroy my soul for what I tell you now,
I'll not let Afrasyab stretch out his claws
Against this prince—not even if he flings
Me to the savage monsters of the deep.'

The next day, when the rising sun displayed   40
Its sword and gloomy night sank down to sleep,
Piran awoke and hurried to the king.
He waited till the court was cleared, then stood
Before the glorious throne and said, 'My lord,
Your splendor shines as does the sun's, you rule
The world, alert and versed in magic arts;
Last night another slave was added to
Your court, his sense seems supernatural,
In beauty he resembles none so much
As you, and if you saw him you would say,   50
"He is a king and there's an end of it."
If Tur could live again, he'd long to see
This prince's face—his face, his hands, his feet,
His glory make him seem like Faridun,
That noble warrior. No man has seen
A fresco painted on a palace wall
Show such a prince, in him the royal glory
Is renewed again. Now cleanse your heart, my lord,

Of evil thoughts; exalt your crown with honour
And in so doing you exalt your heart.'
The brightness of the world's Creator shone
And distanced war, injustice and desires
For vengeance from the soul of Afrasyab.
Grief for the blood of Seyavash worked in
His tortured mind and brought an icy sigh
Up to his lips. Then vehemently he
Regretted what he'd done, the groundless slanders
He'd once believed tormented him. He said,
'I've heard enough about this newborn child
From everyone, and I remember what
The wise men said, that from this boy our days
Will all be filled with war's disturbances;
That from the seed of Tur and Kay Qobad
A king of noble lineage will spring,
The world will seek his patronage and all
The cities of Turan will do him homage.
But now, let what's inevitable come
Since grief and pain and brooding cannot stop it.
Don't keep the boy among your own companions
But send him to the mountains with the shepherds,
So that he'll never know just who he is
Or why he's been entrusted to their care;
He must not learn from anyone the truth
Of his paternity or of the past.'
He said whatever came into his mind,
Thinking he could deceive this ancient earth
As if it were a new and untried world.
(What can you do? The world's not in your hands;
It's vast, beyond your stratagems and hopes;
And if Fate treats you badly now, it is
A teacher pointing out the way to goodness.)
Then happily Piran the champion,
His heart at rest now, blessed the world's Creator,
Praising his sovereign lord he left the court.
He brooded, deep in thought, until he reached
His palace gates, on what would come from all

His kindness and the trouble he'd endured.

He called the shepherds down from Mount Qalun
And talked to them about the baby boy.
He said, 'Take him, preserve this child as if   100
He were your own pure souls, not even dust
Or wind must touch him—you must sacrifice
Your hearts and eyes to ease his way through life.'
He gave the shepherds many gifts and sent
A wet-nurse to accompany them; then he
Entrusted to their care his heart's delight,
The apple of his eye, the noble warrior.
And in this way the turning heavens revolved
And looked on Khosrow with a loving face.
When seven years had passed the warrior's skill   110
And birth were obvious: he made a bow
Of wood and strung it with a length of gut
He'd knotted at each end, and with a blunt
Unfeathered arrow went off to the plains
To hunt. When he was ten he'd grown into
A fearsome fighter able to inflict
His weapon's wounds on boars and bears and wolves;
Thence he progressed to lions and leopards, still
Dependent on that same bent bit of wood.
And so time passed, until the boy refused   120
To take his teacher's orders any longer.
The shepherd came down from the steppe and mountains,
Protesting bitterly to lord Piran:
'I've come to lay before our champion
Complaints concerning this unruly lion;
At first he only hunted deer, he'd no
Desire to fight with lions' or leopards' claws;
Now combat with a lion or chasing deer
Are all the same to him—and God forbid
He should be harmed since you, my noble lord,   130
Will have me hanged!' Piran heard his complaint
And, laughing, said, 'Ability and birth
Will not stay hidden long!' He mounted then

An easy-going horse and rode to see
This lion-cub, Khosrow. Kindly he called
Him to his side and looked him in the face,
And saw the royal glory shining there;
A long time passed while he embraced the boy
And murmured secret prayers for him to God.
140   Then pure-souled Khosrow said to him, 'May you
Illumine all Turan with your great goodness,
Since no one knows or speaks of anything
From you but such benevolence—and look,
You're not ashamed to put your arms around
A shepherd's son!' Piran's wise heart grew hot,
His cheeks flushed red as fire, he said to him,
'You call to mind the chiefs of ancient days,
Deserving of the world, deprived of it!
You are the crown of all the kings; who says
150   That you're the son of shepherds, boy? There is
No shepherd living who is kin to you.
There's much that I could say about all this!'
He ordered royal clothes, and had a horse
And pack-horse brought up for the youth.
The two then travelled to the palace of Piran,
And in his soul Piran mourned Seyavash.
He cherished Khosrow, kept him by his side,
Delighting in his company; time passed
And heaven looked with favor on the prince.

160   One night, about the time for sleep, a man
Arrived from Afrasyab and in the darkness
Summoned Piran to go before the king,
Who spoke at length about the past and said,
'Each night such evil thoughts torment me with
Heart-wrenching grief that it's as if this child
Of Seyavash had darkened all my days.
Can it be fitting for a scion of
Great Faridun to be brought up by shepherds?
And if I'm fated to be harmed by him,
170   There's no avoiding it since God has willed it.

As long as he knows nothing of the past
Let him live happily and I will too—
But if he shows a trace of evil nature,
He'll lose his head, just as his father did.'
Piran replied to him, 'Your Majesty,
You don't need any man to be your teacher:
A little boy with hardly any brains,
What notions can he have about the past?
Don't brood on this, don't take it all so badly.
What did the wise sage say? "The nurse is more 180
Important than the father to a child—
And it's a mother's love that proves decisive."
But first, to set my mind at rest, affirm—
And do it by a royal oath like those
That Faridun once swore, by justice, by
His throne and crown and righteousness—that you'll
Not harm the boy.' When Afrasyab heard this
His animosity was lulled to sleep;
He swore a solemn, binding, royal oath:
'I swear by pallid day and somber night, 190
And by the just Artificer of earth
Who made the sky, the beasts, the human soul,
That this young child shall never suffer wrong
From me, no, not so much as by my breath.'
Piran then kissed the ground and said, 'O king,
Unrivalled and unequalled in your justice,
Your oath has reassured me and my soul
Is now at peace.' From there he hurried back
To see Khosrow, his face all flushed, his heart
Suffused with happiness. He said to him, 200
'Now exile wisdom from your heart: if he
Should talk to you of battles, make your answer
Banquets: act like a fool in front of him,
And when you talk make sure you're talking nonsense,
If you can speak and give no hint of wisdom,
With luck you'll live to see another day.'
He placed the royal crown upon his head
And bound the royal belt about his waist,

Then had a trim, high-stepping horse brought out
210   For him; the pure, well-meaning warrior mounted,
And all the world looked on and wept as they
Approached the court of Afrasyab. A shout
Rose, 'Clear the way, a new king comes to court!'
Piran led in the princely warrior
To Afrasyab, his grandfather, whose cheeks
Grew wet with shame. He stared a long while at
The youth's strong neck and hands and arms, his might
And royal glory; as he gazed his face
Lost all its color, and Piran began
220   To tremble like a willow tree, afraid
Now for the young man's life. There was a pause.
And Fate filled all the monarch's heart with kindness:
His face relaxed. He asked, 'Young man, what's your
Experience of this world? How do you tend
Your sheep? How do you pasture them, and where?'
He answered, 'There's no hunting, I've no bow
Or feathers to my arrows.' Then he asked
About his teacher and the good and bad
That Fate had given him. He said, 'Where there's
230   A leopard, sharp claws tear the hearts of men.'
Thirdly he questioned him about his parents,
His home and town, and how he ate and slept.
He answered him, 'A nasty cur can't bring
A ravening lion down.'[84] Then Afrasyab
Laughed at his words and, turning to Piran,
Said, 'He's a half-wit: when I ask about
The head his answer's all to do with feet!
No good or evil can be got from him,
And men like this don't meditate revenge.
240   Find someone sensible to take him to
His mother; send him back to Seyavashkard,
And keep him clear of evil counselors;
Provide him with whatever he might need—
Attendants, horses, cash and all the rest.'
Piran was quick to hurry Khosrow from
The audience chamber: since the evil eye

Seemed sealed he came back to his home rejoicing.
He said, 'God in His justice has bestowed
A new tree on the world, and now it gives   250
The world its fruitful crop.' He opened wide
His treasury's portals and equipped the prince
With all he needed—cash and rich brocades,
Swords, jewels, horses, purses filled with coins, thrones,
Crowns, carpets, armor, belts and all the rest.
He sent Khosrow and Farigis to where
The city Seyavash had built once stood;
The site was now a wilderness of thorns.
But when they reached there men from every quarter
Gathered and bowed down to the ground in homage,
The very beasts made their obeisance to him,   260
And every man who'd any virtue said,
'Thanks be to God Who rules the world that from
The noble tree's uprooted stock He's brought
This shoot forth; may the evil eye not strike
The royal prince, may Seyavash's soul
Be filled with light.' Then in that ruined city
The soil began to flower, the weeds became
Tall cypresses, and from the dust that drank
The blood of Seyavash a tree rose up
To touch the clouds; each leaf displayed his likeness,   270
And from his love there came the scent of musk.
It was an evergreen that flourished in
December's cold as freshly as in springtime,
A place where those who mourned for Seyavash
Would gather and bewail his death and worship.

Such is the way this ancient crone we call
The earth will act: she pulls the mother's breast
Back from the suckling child, and when the heart
Has learnt to love the world she drags the head
Down—suddenly—into the dust. But give   280
Yourself to joy, and in the garden of
This world avoid the scent of sorrow's leaves;
For whether you are crowned or live in want,

Your life will not be long. Do not torment
Your soul, this world is not your dwelling-place,
All you inherit is a narrow bier.
Why strain and strive and struggle? Sit and eat,
And put your trust in treasure that is God's.

TRANSLATOR'S AFTERWORD

When news of the death of Seyavash reached Iran the court went into mourning. Rostam dragged Sudabeh from the harem and killed her for her part in Seyavash's downfall. He then invaded Turan and laid much of it waste. With the help of Piran and the Iranian warrior Giv, Khosrow and his mother reached Iran. Kavus handed the reins of power over to Khosrow. Rostam and Khosrow sought revenge for the death of Seyavash and after lengthy battles were finally victorious over the armies of Turan; a particularly tragic episode of the war involved Forud, the son of Jarireh and Seyavash, who was killed by Tus, despite Khosrow's express orders to the contrary. Piran was killed defending his country and so was Afrasyab, when he was finally captured.

Khosrow ruled as an exemplary and just king. After the death of Kavus he announced his intention to resign the throne, as he feared the hubris absolute power brings with it. He had no sons and nominated a hitherto unknown warrior, Lohrasp, as his successor, to the consternation of Rostam and Zal. Despite their objections he went forward with his plan to abdicate: he retired to a mountain fastness, followed by his most trusted advisers, and disappeared from their view in a snowstorm.

Lohrasp became king, and the old connection between Sistan (where Rostam's family ruled) and the Persian court began to break down. Lohrasp's son Goshtasp sent his son Esfandyar to enslave Rostam. Rostam reluctantly killed Esfandyar; he was himself killed by his own brother, Shaghad, and the rest of his family were wiped out by Esfandyar's son Bahman.

Bahman married his daughter Homai (see note 10 to the main text); their son (Darab) was committed to the Euphrates in a basket (why is not really made plain) and brought up by peasants. He later learnt about his birth and was crowned by his mother. He married the daughter of 'Filqus' (Philip) of Greece but was offended by her and sent her back to Greece, where she bore their son Eskandar (Alexander the Great). Eskandar grew up to defeat Darab's other son (by a Persian wife) Dara, and thus became lord of Iran. With the advent of Eskandar the legendary portion of the poem draws to a close; the poet compresses five hundred years into one reign and passes on to the Sasanian, 'historical', closing section.

NOTES

1 'i Persiani attuali lo considerano il simbolo dell'iranismo, il padre
   della patria' (Letteratura persiana, Milan, 1960, p. 589)
2 Whether the name 'Iran or 'Persia' should be used is a ques-
   tion that can arouse considerable anger. The Western usage of
   Iran stems from the decree by Reza Shah in 1935 that this (the
   name of the country in Persian) was how the country was to be
   known: until then, the English name had always been Persia. The
   egregious ignorance demonstrated by this attempt to tell other
   people how to speak their own languages ('Persia' is a word in
   the English language just as 'Alman' [Germany] and 'Lahestan
   [Poland] are words in the Persian language) may have been de-
   plorable, nevertheless it has had its effect and 'Iran' is now almost
   universally used. In the translation of Seyavash I have on the
   whole used 'Iran' and 'Iranian' though occasionally I give 'Persia'
   and 'Persian' (as a translator of Homer might use both 'Hellas/
   Hellenic' and 'Greece/Greek').
3 Some one thousand lines are by Ferdowsi's predecessor Daqiqi:
   Ferdowsi took over the task of writing the poem when Daqiqi
   was murdered by a slave. Daqiqi had begun in medias res (with
   the advent of Zoroastrianism), but Ferdowsi begins at the beginning, with the creation of the world. Daqiqi's portion is therefore
   an episode embedded in the middle of what is overwhelmingly
   Ferdowsi's poem.
4 If this name looks vaguely familiar to a Western reader, it is probably because of Puccini's Turandot, a word which is a corruption
   of the Persian 'turandokht', meaning 'girl (princess) of Turan,'
   Turan being central Asia.
5 Perhaps because of Arnold's poem this has been the most frequently translated episode of The Shahnameh. The best English
   translation is that by Jerome Clinton (University of Washington
   Press, Seattle, 1987).
6 Kavus is succeeded by his grandson Khosrow. However, for most
   of Khosrow's reign Kavus is still alive and Khosrow refers back
   to him as the ultimate authority. When Kavus dies Khosrow is

crowned again, as if confirming that it is only then that he does really become king, and a couple of lines later he announces his intention to abdicate. If we count Kavus's reign as lasting till his death, Ferdowsi gives him more space than any other king; if we count it only until Khosrow becomes regent, he is still one of the most extensively treated kings of the poem.

7   e.g. the stories of Zahhak and Kaveh; Kavus, Rostam and Sohrab; Goshtasp, Rostam and Esfandyar.

8   It is unfortunate for a modern audience that the only signifi-cant female character in the Seyavash episode is Sudabeh, who is a lustful scheming and vindictive stepmother. Though *The Shahnameh,* as an epic poem, records a primarily male world, it does, in fact, include very sympathetic portraits of women—in particular Manizheh and Gordiyeh, both of whom display loy-alty and heroism when the menfolk who might be expected to display such virtues fail. The Turanian princess Manizheh de-fies Afrasyab to protect her Iranian lover Bizhan, keeping him alive when Afrasyab has him thrown into a dark well and she has become for Persian myth the archetype of loyalty in adversity. Gordiyeh opposes her brother Bahram Chubineh in his attempt to wrest the Iranian throne from the legitimate heir Khosrow Parviz, and her spirited speeches in defense of the poem's epic values are among the most moving and eloquent in the whole work.

9   A closer parallel for Ferdowsi and his original Islamic audience would be the story of Yusuf and Zuleikha from the Koran (Joseph and Potiphar's wife in the Bible); again an attempt is made on the chastity of a young man seen as a spiritual hero/victim, and when her overtures are rejected the scorned woman accuses the young man before her husband of having tried to seduce/rape her. Interestingly enough, there is an eleventh-century Persian poem on the Yusuf and Zuleikha story which used to be ascribed to Ferdowsi, though scholars now reject the attribution: it may be that it was its broad similarity to parts of Ferdowsi's treatment of the Seyavash story that led to the ascription in the first place.

10 Specifically the Histories of Tabari (about a century before Ferdowsi's work, and therefore available to him as a source) and of Tha'alebi (about fifty years after Ferdowsi's work).

11 'Persian Jones', as he was called, author of the first Persian gram-mar in English (1771) and the first man to suggest the existence of the Indo-European family of languages including Latin, Greek,

Persian and Sanskrit—the intuition that such a relationship existed is said to have come to him while reading *The Shahnameh*.

12 It was largely from Mohl's French version that Matthew Arnold learnt of the Sohrab and Rostam story, though he seems also to have known Atkinson's version.

THE LEGEND OF SEYAVASH

1 This paraphrases and glosses the word *'dehqan'* ('chief man or magistrate of a village, prince or head of the farmers', according to Steingass's dictionary). Ferdowsi himself belonged to this class, which saw itself as the repository of Persian legend and history. The same *dehqan* is mentioned in the penultimate line of the introduction to the Seyavash story, and again I have added the gloss of him as collector of tales.

2 The Zoroastrian priesthood was the learned and conservative component of pre-Islamic Iranian society and was seen as having the most direct access to ancient tradition. The mention of a 'priest of Zoroaster' would therefore give more authority to tales from that period.

3 Turan was loosely conceived of as the area to the north of the river Oxus, the land of the Turks who were the traditional enemies of Iran in *The Shahnameh*. The Turks' of *The Shahnameh* were central Asians, not people living in the area covered by modern Turkey.

4 Faridun was a legendary king who ruled all the world. He divided the world between his three sons, Iraj, Tur and Salm, and, as in Lear's case, only the youngest child was worthy of his father's trust. Tur received Asia (hence its name Turan), Salm the West, and Iraj, the youngest, was given the prize share, Iran. Jealous of their brother's portion, Tur and Salm conspired against him and murdered him, thereby marking the beginning of the long enmity between Iran and Turan, which is renewed by the murder of Seyavash, a hero who has much in common with Iraj.

5 According to a disputed reading in the Koran, Azar was the father of Abraham, and lived by carving idols. The name became proverbial in Persian poetry for an idolater or for a maker of something beautiful.

6 The use of the bow and lariat is included among the skills of horsemanship because both were normally used when the warrior was

mounted, rather than on foot. This is clear in the contests of skill that appear later in the poem.

7 This means 'mountainous country'. It is not clear if 'Kuhestan' is being used as a synonym for 'Khorasan' (parts of which are notably mountainous), or if it refers to a second area that has been granted to Seyavash. Copyists of the poem attempted to resolve the ambiguity by adding a line identifying the second area as Transoxiana. This seems wrong, as Transoxiana is the homeland of the Turanians, under their king Afrasyab. Various parts of Iran have been called 'Kuhestan' at different times, but during Ferdowsi's own lifetime the area immediately to the south and south-east of Khorasan (through which the modern Iran-Afghanistan border runs) was so called, and it is probably to this area that Ferdowsi is referring.

8 This is again a difficult crux: the phrase seems to mean 'from the place that the high sun makes worthy [i.e. illuminates] the dust' and this, as Minovi says, implies a balancing phrase, indicating a second place (the sentence as it stands implies 'from this place that the sun makes worthy *to* some other place'), which is absent. Minovi remarks that the phrase seems to have little to do with the previous line, but if we take the one as a metaphor for the other (the king equals the sun, Seyavash is the dust made worthy by the sun's rays, a metaphor very much within the spirit of *The Shahnameh*'s rhetoric), then there is a valid connection between the two lines and the need for a balancing phrase is eliminated.

9 Sudabeh has praised Seyavash; praising the young can still, in contemporary Iran, be considered as possibly attracting a malign revenge from Fate, or 'the evil eye'.

10 Royal incest (brother/sister, father/daughter) was not uncommon and, as in the royal dynasties of ancient Egypt, was even considered preferable to marriage outside the family. There are indications of such incestuous marriages in the Sasanian section that closes *The Shahnameh*, and the plot of the poem *Vis and Ramin* (by Gorgani, composed a little later than *The Shahnameh*), which preserves pre-Islamic customs more than any other medieval Iranian poem, involves a sanctioned royal brother/sister incest.

11 This prince will be Kay Khosrow, the greatest king of the poem's legendary section. Astrologers' predictions are always correct in *The Shahnameh*.

12 This is an idiom, still used in modern Persian, meaning hypocrisy, or (as here) a hidden danger.

13 It is not clear if this means her daughters, or the women of the harem in general (the Persian word can mean 'girl' or 'daughter'). Piran and Sudabeh herself say she has more than one daughter, but later when Seyavash is to ask for her daughter's hand, which daughter is not specified and it seems that there is only one.

14 A town in central Asia proverbial for the beauty of its women.

15 The name of a country, here used to mean its king. The king of Hamaveran is Sudabeh's father, who imprisoned Kavus when he came asking for Sudabeh's hand. Though Sudabeh was faithful to her husband against her father during this episode and ministered to him during his imprisonment, Seyavash's point is 'like father like daughter', and he believes that Sudabeh cannot be trusted to further Iranian, or his own, interests.

16 Literally 'marrow and skin'.

17 The text is uncertain at this point; I have followed the version that appears in the Moscow edition of Bertel's *et al.*

18 i.e. never.

19 See note 16.

20 The line appears to be corrupt; the English indicates the meaning that seems the most likely to have been intended.

21 'Tears of blood' is a common phrase in *The Shahnameh*. Because of its slightly peculiar quality in English I have usually rendered it by 'desperate tears'. In his translation of the Turkish *Book of Dede Korkut* (Penguin, 1974), which makes use of the same expression, Geoffrey Lewis comments, 'This is not entirely metaphorical, for at Turkish funerals in ancient times the mourners would gash their faces and let the blood mingle with their tears', and we have seen how Sudabeh had indeed gashed her face here. Burton *(The Anatomy of Melancholy,* Pt. 3, Sec. 2, Mem. 2, Subs. 3) quotes a Western Latin parallel *'sanguines lacrimis deplorandum,* saith Matenesius, and with tears of blood to be deplored'.

22 The line is questionable; this seems the most likely meaning.

23 A parasang is about three to four miles. Traditionally explained as the journey a laden pack-animal could travel in an hour, and therefore varying with the roughness of the terrain.

24 This would be considered a sign of his readiness for death, as the corpses of the illustrious were sprinkled with camphor.

25 The word 'roof' is translated from Mohl's text; it is absent from Minovi's.

26 Kayanid was the name of Kavus's dynasty.

27 The ox-headed mace was a symbol of kingship, first mentioned in

the poem in connection with the mythological king Faridun.

28 Zal has been brought up by the fabulous bird the simorg, under whose magical protection he and his family live. His son is Rostam, who has reared Seyavash, and Sudabeh is implying that Rostam and Zal have protected their ward by magic.

29 In the translations of Mohl and the Warners, this speech is given to Sudabeh and addressed to Seyavash. I think it more likely to be meant for Kavus and addressed to Sudabeh.

30 Literally 'pouring blood', but the 'blood' here as elsewhere clearly refers to tears—see note 21.

31 The references are to Kavus's campaign against the demons inhabiting Mazanderan and to his being captured by his father-in-law, the king of Hamaveran. On both occasions he was rescued from the results of his own rashness by Rostam.

32 Rostam's horse, of fabulous speed, strength and sagacity.

33 A commonly mentioned form of wealth in *The Shahnameh*. The Iranian plateau and its civilizations have been known for the production of fine cloth from prehistoric times to the present century.

34 Kaveh was the blacksmith hero of the populist Iranian revolt against the demon king Zahhak early in the *Shahnameh*. His banner was his leather blacksmith's apron, later adopted as a royal banner by the just king Faridun and his successors, of whom Kavus is one. The banner glitters because it was decorated by Faridun and then by each successive king with jewels.

35 These seem something of an unlikely anachronism in a pre-Islamic war fought across the Oxus. However, it is known that elephants were used by the Sasanians, as the Arab historians who described the defeat of the Persian forces in the seventh century mention the destruction caused by their routed elephants. There is even some evidence that they were present at the Battle of Gaugamela, when Alexander the Great defeated the Achaemenids, though this is disputed. Elsewhere in the text Rostam's horse, Rakhsh, is referred to metaphorically as an elephant because of its strength, and it may be that the original usage in the poem was in many places metaphorical. Nevertheless, by the time the poem came to be illustrated by miniaturists, the references to elephants were taken literally, and Ferdowsi himself may well have envisaged actual elephants—his sources drawing on Sasanian tradition.

36 Rostam's home territory, also called Sistan, which seems to have been roughly coterminous with the south-west of modern

Afghanistan. A march from Khorasan to Balkh (where the battles of the campaign are fought) would have involved something of a detour through this area, and, as often in *The Shahnameh,* the geography is rather hazy. Certainly, an excursion into India, as is mentioned a few lines later, would take Seyavash and Rostam well out of their way, and having them then pass through Herat would make them double back on themselves.

37 Some texts omit the reference to the harem, presumably because the copyists felt it was not compatible with Seyavash's determinedly chaste intentions as established by the episodes in Kavus's harem.

38 This was meant for the enemies whom he would slaughter. 'Holding a shroud' means 'bringing death'.

39 Afrasyab, the king of Turan, whose inhabitants are conceived of as central Asian Turks.

40 Garsivaz interprets by adducing the opposite of the obvious meaning, a common way of explaining dreams.

41 See note 4.

42 Presumably it took a day to get all the gifts across.

43 This would be either for not coming out to meet him, or for defeating him before Balkh, where Garsivaz commanded the army of Turan.

44 Kavus gives frequent examples of his anger throughout his reign. The most spectacular is against Rostam himself, when he threatens to have the champion killed for his delay in response to a summons to appear at court.

45 Afrasyab had overrun Iran and killed its king, Nozar.

46 The name for the evil principle of the universe.

47 Qobad was the king who restored Iran's fortunes after the murder of Nozar; he was the father of Kavus and therefore the grandfather of Seyavash.

48 See note 15. Sudabeh is seen here as the cause of Seyavash's misfortunes.

49 This would reverse the normal practice, according to which a son stood before the father as a sign of readiness to serve him.

50 Literally 'To "shut" he is the same, to "open" he is the same'—i.e. whatever I do he is opposed to it.

51 Seyavash has already passed through this town some thirty lines previously; either this is an oversight of Ferdowsi's, or the text is corrupt.

52 They are cousins.

53 This line appears to be corrupt and is marked as such in Minovi's text. Adopting the slightly different reading of some texts (reading the word *'dur'* [far] for *'dud'* [smoke]), it seems to mean 'you will experience from afar the remedy for this poison', and I have assumed that this is more or less the intended meaning. This fits Seyavash's reproach to Piran when he is later apparently abandoned by him.

54 Mohl takes 'Turan's great general' to refer to Piran; however, Afrasyab is often called Turan's general *('sepahbod')* and it seems likely that the king is here referring to himself.

55 Polo was originally a Persian/central Asian game; it was taken to India by the Moghuls and from thence (via the British raj) to the West. The Afghani Bozkashi (in which a goat takes the place of the ball) is a variant or ancestor of the game.

56 Pahlavi was the name of the ancient language of Persia. Presumably Seyavash calls out in Pahlavi so that Afrasyab will not understand.

57 This is an awkward transition. We are probably meant to envisage Piran returning to his own castle after chatting with Seyavash and then going back to Seyavash the next morning. It might be, though, that the text is defective at this point. There is evidence that Ferdowsi produced at least two versions of *The Shahnameh* and we may have here a first version and a revision both finding their ways into the same text, as has happened for example in some of Shakespeare's plays (e.g. *Romeo and Juliet* V, iii; *Love's Labour's Lost* V, ii).

58 Golshahr is here introduced as if for the first time, although we have already met her during the preparations for the marriage of her daughter Jarireh to Seyavash. Another peculiarity is that it seems to be from their own house that Golshahr and Piran provide Farigis's dowry, rather than from the king's. It may be that there was at some point in the development of the story only one marriage and that this accounts for the slight awkwardness here. The text of the historian Tha'alebi, whose very summary treatment of the story is in general close to Ferdowsi's, is somewhat ambiguous about how many wives Seyavash has and does not mention Jarireh.

59 Here approximately fifty-four lines of the older printed editions of the text are omitted, in accordance with recent scholarship which has labeled them a later interpolation.

60 Meaning 'Seyavash made it' or 'the work of Seyavash'; this reading

follows Minovi's text. Most texts give 'Seyavashgerd', meaning 'Seyavash's city'.

61 Literally, the day of 'Ard'—the name of the twenty-fifth day of each Zoroastrian month, which was considered auspicious.

62 The gate-keeper and gardener of the Muslim paradise. Ferdowsi occasionally slips into religious anachronisms like this. More usual is his ascribing Zoroastrian practices to the pre-Zoroastrian period, to which, according to his poem's scheme, the story of Seyavash belongs (Zoroastrianism is introduced in the poem under king Goshtasp, who rules three generations after the death of Kavus).

63 An angel. The text seems corrupt during Piran's speech (Minovi suggests that a line has been lost), and I've slightly rearranged the lines to make the general sense clearer.

64 Literally, 'You'd say that mind mixed with wisdom.' Wisdom, in Ferdowsi, seems to be conceived of as a quasi-divine entity or substance (there is a passage in praise of it at the poem's opening) with which men can enter into a relationship. The usual way of expressing this is to say that a man marries, or couples with, wisdom. By saying that Seyavash's mind mixes with this entity the poet implies that his mind is in the closest possible relationship with a quasi-divine intelligence. This is perhaps analogous to the great twelfth-century Spanish Muslim Neoplatonic philosopher Ibn Rushd's notion of a universal and quasi-divine mind. Ibn Rushd (known in the West as Averroes) believed that 'man's destiny is to rise by degrees to that intellectual or immaterial condition proper to . . . the active intellect . . . The token of this extraterrestrial condition is the fully actualized capacity of the mind to apprehend intelligible forms directly, without any intermediaries, and to apprehend itself as well.' (Majid Fakhry, *A History of Islamic Philosophy*, Columbia University Press, New York and London, 1970, pp. 324–5).

65 Jarireh, Piran's daughter and the wife of Seyavash.

66 Well into the twentieth century the bearer of news that a boy had been born was rewarded with a present, often money; on the other hand no one was eager to pass on news that a girl had been born as the messenger was unlikely to receive any reward.

67 The ancient form of Persian wrestling, which could be practiced on foot or on horseback, involved grasping the opponent's belt in order to throw him. There are miniatures of *The Shahnameh* which show two warriors facing each other, their hands gripping

each other's belt and straining to throw one another.

68 This was the name of a temple where the Zoroastrian sacred flame was kept in Sasanian Iran. The point of comparing Garsivaz's helmet to the temple is obviously, in general, that it is far superior to Seyavash's, though the exact point of the comparison is not clear. It may be simply in terms of its height or strength; Mohl in his French translation suggests the helmet is as sacred as the temple is to Seyavash. This is by the way another example of Ferdowsi's frequent anachronisms as regards Zoroastrianism—the advent of which he places three generations after Seyavash's tale. The prince's reluctance to wrestle with Garsivaz echoes his reluctance to play polo against Afrasyab and his call to the Persians to let the Turks win in their contests—he doesn't want to show his hosts up as inferior to himself.

69 In *The Shahnameh* Iraj (see note 4) is a very similar figure to Seyavash—a well-meaning innocent whose murder initiates a long series of wars—and the two are frequently compared with one another. Garsivaz's point here is that the enmity between Turan and Iran is traditional, and Afrasyab cannot overcome it by friendship with Seyavash. However, by drawing attention to Iraj and his fate he recalls to the poem's audience the parallel of Iraj and Seyavash as innocents, and casts himself in the role of the envious Tur.

70 The meaning at this point is not wholly clear. The lion-cub is Seyavash (who is elsewhere compared to a lion-cub who may harm Afrasyab if he gives it shelter), but the exact application of the metaphor here is vague. Minovi suggests that the lines imply 'If the lion-cub [Seyavash] seeks shelter and I harm him though he is innocent of harming me, will God approve of this?', and I have followed this suggestion in phrasing the translation.

71 'and with no flock there can't/Be any shepherd': there are almost as many differing versions of this line as there are manuscripts; I have taken the one that seems to make the most sense in the context.

72 For Seyavash not to welcome Afrasyab's brother by going out to meet him would be a deadly insult, and Garsivaz wishes to be able to report that he—and by implication Afrasyab—has been insulted in this way. This practice of sending out or accompanying a party to greet a dignitary and of indicating the respect in which he or she was held by the size of the party continued well into the nineteenth century. The insufferable Curzon was very

punctilious about the size of the reception committees sent out to meet him when he was traveling in Persia.

73 The Persian word for 'Royal Glory' is '*farr*', a term referring to a splendor possessed only by those fit to rule and conferred by God. It can be forfeited by those who abuse their power, as Tur does. In *The Shahnameh* the attribute is restricted to members of the Iranian and Turanian royal families and occasionally to client kings like Rostam.

74 The metaphor, a formula in *The Shahnameh,* means 'the end of this [his] business is as yet unknown' (Nushin).

75 Aghriras was Afrasyab's brother, killed by him after a disagreement as to what to do with Iranian prisoners. The fratricide echoes the Tur-Iraj quarrel (like Iraj, Aghriras is presented as modest and unassuming and is sympathetic to the Iranian cause); the quarrel over what to do with enemies within your power foreshadows the Seyavash-Kavus argument over the hostages from Turan.

76 The line is obscure and has been interpreted in differing ways. I think the key to it is that the phrase 'being engulfed by the dragon's breath' is an expression for an eclipse, and refers back to Seyavash's claim that his heart shines brighter than the sun in heaven (and also to the implied 'eclipse' of Afrasyab's heart, likened to a darkened moon); since the purity of his heart is uneclipsed by evil (the dragon's breath) he believes God will not abandon him.

77 This phrase is not in the text, but it is evident from the intervention of Farigis below that the scene which follows takes place at or close to Seyavashkard.

78 Zahhak is the first evil person to appear in the poem. He revolted against his father and against his king, Jamshid, both of whom he killed. He ruled Iran as a tyrant and was defeated by Faridun. The story of Salm and Tur has been told above (see note 4). Farigis's point is that the murderers of kings themselves come to a sticky end because their crimes will provoke revenge.

79 This sentence (two lines of verse) is absent from Minovi's text; it is however present in other texts and as Minovi points out it is present in the Arabic translation by Bondari, which precedes all extant Persian texts and which is normally taken as a good guide to the reliability or otherwise of the Persian manuscripts.

80 The sun is Seyavash's head, the cypress tree his body, both expressions being formulaic in *The Shahnameh* and in the poetry of the period generally. The rhetoric that follows, 'may there never be

a sun or cypress again', is perhaps alien in feeling to the English poetic tradition and difficult to convey; a near equivalent might be Shakespeare's Cleopatra's 'The odds is gone,/ And there is nothing left remarkable/ Beneath the visiting moon' *(Antony and Cleopatra,* IV, xv, 66–8).

81 The Warners have a note to the effect that this means a remount for each man, since five (Piran, Ruin, Farshidvard, Lahhak, Pilsom) will be making the journey.

82 We have a double time-scheme here: the scene when Lahhak and Pilsom left for Piran's court has been, as it were, in suspended animation till their return.

83 She accuses Piran because he had arranged her marriage with Seyavash.

84 Minovi's text has 'will bring', not 'can't bring', though as he notes most texts have a negative here. I have preferred the negative because, though Khosrow's answers are probably meant to be nothing more than nonsense, it is possible that they are meant as a disguised commentary on his own situation. As the future king of Iran threatened by Afrasyab, Khosrow would be identified with the lion and Afrasyab with the quarrelsome dog, and the negative, implying that Afrasyab will not destroy Khosrow, therefore seems the more likely.

CPSIA information can be obtained at www.ICGtesting.com
Printed in the USA
LVOW10s0831260713

344465LV00001B/2/A